BOOK TOWNS

F FRANCES
LINCOLN

BOOK TOWNS

FORTY-FIVE PARADISES OF THE PRINTED WORD

ALEX JOHNSON

For Philip and Phyllis, Wilma,
Thomas, Edward and Robert

CONTENTS

INTRODUCTION

Sometimes you need more than just one book, more than just one bookshop. Sometimes you need a whole book town.

Whether you call it a Boekenstad, Village du Livres, Bokby or Bókabæirnir, from Canada to Korea and from Iceland to Australia a movement is growing. In hamlets, villages and towns around the world, like-minded booksellers, calligraphers, bookbinders, curators, publishers and architects are coming together to ensure a future for the printed book, defying the e-book onslaught, and providing a new future for fading communities.

This is the first book to bring all of these book towns together, offering a unique history of each one, and encouraging readers to seek them out. By visiting these towns you are not only helping to save the printed book; you are helping to keep communities alive.

A book town is simply a small town, usually rural and scenic, full of bookshops and book-related industries. The movement started with Richard Booth in Hay-on-Wye in Wales in the 1960s (see page 65), picked up speed in the 1980s and is continuing to thrive in the new millennium. From the start, the driving force has been to encourage sustainable tourism and help regenerate communities faced with economic collapse and soaring unemployment. One important reason that almost all book towns are in bucolic locations is that they require cheap property to enable book businesses to open their doors. Many have been subsidised by local authorities to help them get off the ground.

While many cities have numerous bookshops, book towns concentrate the outlets in a small area to create a critical mass. There are some sellers such as Barter Books in Alnwick, England, or the late Tom Rudloff's Antiquarium in Brownville, Nebraska, which are their town's main attraction; but however impressive they are to visit, they do not make their location a book town. Booktown Books in Grass Valley, California, is somewhere in-between – a remarkable co-operative of a dozen booksellers who work out of a large two-storey building.

And while most are run by individual booksellers, some have taken a different route. Purgstall (population: 5,000) in Lower Austria is the country's only book town, an hour west of Vienna by train or road. Established in 2000, it is run as a non-profit organisation by a team of volunteers who also aim to provide opportunities for people who are ill or disabled. Despite a bad fire in 2013, Purgstall is still keen to cater for people who enjoy books and in 2016 installed two renovated telephone boxes as *Bücherschränke* (honesty libraries) in the church square.

The results of the book town crusaders have been impressive. By rebranding themselves, they are attracting more visitors who then stay in the local hotels and guesthouses, dine in the local eateries, go shopping in the town shops and gradually rebuild the local economy. Some even end up buying property. A visitor to Wigtown in Scotland in 1988 who returned today would barely recognise it.

Book towns also create more voices in support of the printed word, in a time of technological flux. While encouraging 'old-fashioned' book buying, they have also helped centuries-old techniques such as papermaking to flourish, with positive knock-on effects on other creative industries locally, particularly for artists. At the same time, many of these sellers have also harnessed the power of the internet to run their businesses partly online (though several are resolutely opposed to this). Several have developed major literary festivals; Hay-on-Wye's is the most famous, but almost all book towns have their own. Võtikvere book village in Estonia may have no booksellers, but that does not stop it running an annual literary gathering each August, organised by writer Imbi Paju to celebrate literature and books.

Although they all operate independently, many are members of the International Organisation of Book Towns (even though some are more of a bookshop quarter than an actual township). The IOBT aims to raise interest in the book town ethos and runs a biennial festival in one of the member towns.

Inevitably not all book towns have stayed the course. Blaenavon in Wales and Atherstone in England had the misfortune to be very closely involved with an individual who is now serving a long prison sentence in America, and their book town projects subsequently fell by the wayside (although the enormous Astley Book Farm, a dozen miles from Atherstone, is keeping book buying alive in the area).

Others have started hopefully but never taken off. Writer Larry McMurtry hoped that his vast shop, Booked Up, would kickstart plans to turn Archer City in Texas into a book town. Sadly these plans have faded, and his own bookselling empire has shrunk. In Stillwater, Minnesota, the closure of St. Croix Antiquarian Books leaves only Loome Theological Booksellers and Valley

Bookseller to keep the flame alive (see page 132). In Germany, Edenkoben is no longer a *Bücherdorf*, although there is still a rather nice book café there, Bäckerei & Büchercafe Dicker, if you're passing nearby.

But on the bright side, new locations are in the pipeline. Indian authorities have recently begun what they hope will become a 'book village' network, and El Pedroso in Andalucia, Spain, is a prospective member of the IOBT. There is talk of a 'Borneo Book Village'; an integrated book centre in Kuching in the near future. And some that looked like they were on their way out, such as Bowral in Australia, have happily returned with a new lease of life (see page 28).

At a time when libraries are becoming an endangered species and independent bookshops struggle against the rise of the e-book, book towns are beacons of hope in the fight to keep the traditional book alive. Please visit them and buy a book or two.

Left: Outdoor honesty bookshops like this one in Hay-on-Wye, Wales are common sights in book towns around the world.

Right: Wise words for anyone visiting a book town, here painted on a shopfront in Hay-on-Wye.

Note
The opening hours of the bookshops and other book businesses in book towns varies tremendously. They are usually open at weekends and during holidays, though even this varies, while others operate normal weekday business hours as well. Please do check times before visiting to avoid disappointment.

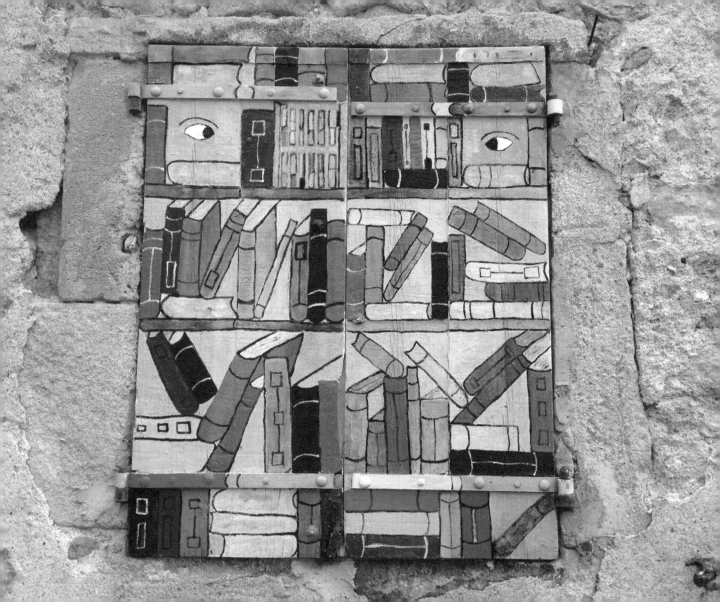

BOOK TOWNS

Playful painted window shutters appeal to younger readers in Montolieu, France.

In the wilderness of South Africa; amid the beauty of the Norwegian fjords; on the border of the Korean Demilitarized Zone. Across the globe, secondhand bookshops, publishers and printmakers have huddled together to form unique havens of literature. The following pages form a guide to the best.

ASCONA
SWITZERLAND

The community hosted a great number of artists, writers and philosophers; among them Hermann Hesse, Erich Maria Remarque, Isadora Duncan and Rudolf Steiner.

Ascona lakeside at night.

Ascona, Switzerland's lowest lying town, is right on the northern shore of Lake Maggiore – a cosmopolitan spot popular with tourists in the Italian-speaking Canton of Ticino. The old town with its labyrinth of cobbled lanes dates back to the sixteenth century, and has been beautifully restored. Indeed, Ascona is listed as a town of national importance on the Inventory of Swiss Heritage Sites. It is also a member of the International Organisation of Book Towns.

At the start of the twentieth century an artists' colony was established on the town's Monte Verità (Hill of Truth), focusing on the benefits of nature, naturism and vegetarianism. The community hosted a great number of artists, writers and philosophers; among them Hermann Hesse, Erich Maria Remarque, Isadora Duncan and Rudolf Steiner.

Ascona's leading bookshop is the historic Libreria della Rondine (Piazza san Pietro), founded by Amsterdam-born Leo Kok, a musician and pacifist. He survived the Buchenwald concentration camp, but the torture he endured there ended his career as a pianist. When he was freed, Kok opened a secondhand bookshop in Ascona, covering several floors in the beautiful seventeenth-century palazzo Casa Serodine, initially using his own personal library as stock. He ran it from 1946 until 1979, and as well as a bookshop (specialising in German texts), it became a meeting place for German-speaking artists and intellectuals. The Libreria Ascona on Via Borgo also has a good collection of books in German, as well as English, Italian and French.

The Centro del Bel Libro Ascona (Via Collegio) is another important landmark. This leading institute runs courses for both professionals and amateurs on all aspects of book production – from papermaking and conservation to slipcases, book design and leather bookbinding. Founded in 1965 by Josef Stemmle, it is now run by the multilingual Suzanne Schmollgruber.

Ascona's town library, the Biblioteca Popolare, was founded by American Charlotte Giese in 1926 on the lovely lakeside promenade (Piazza Giuseppe Motta), and has excellent views. Among the town's other attractions are a major annual jazz festival and a historic mini-golf course.

Eventi Letterari Monte Verità

This relatively new annual literary festival continues the town's tradition of artistic events and communities. It is held at the Monte Verità Conference and Cultural Centre and other locations around town including the Teatro San Materno, Piazza Elvezia and the Ascona Public Library. While it attracts major authors such as Ian McEwan and Orhan Pamuk to its programmes, the festival also concentrates on giving a platform to younger writers. Each festival has a theme such as 'Utopia and memory' and 'Love in all its forms'.

Readings are performed in the native language of the respective author, but are mostly simultaneously translated into Italian, German and French. A day ticket is 30 Swiss Francs (there are also concessions), with single event and full festival passes also available.

A key part of the festival is its all day open-air book market on the lake promenade of Ascona. As well as new and secondhand books, you can find objects made of wood and paper, handbags made of old books, and local culinary delicacies.

More information
- Libreria della Rondine – www.larondine.ch
- Centro del Bel Libro – www.cbl-ascona.ch
- www.eventiletterari.ch
- The nearest train station is in the nearby town of Locarno, which is around twenty minutes away by car (although the centre is largely pedestrianised). There are also frequent buses connecting the two towns.

Left: Outside Casa Serodine and La Rondine, looking down towards the lake.

Opposite above left: The Monte Verità Conference and Cultural Centre.

Opposite below left: The Centro del Bel Libro Ascona.

Opposite above right: Libreria Ascona on Via Borgo.

Opposite below right: A student hard at work on a bookbinding course at the Centro del Bel Libro Ascona.

BECHEREL
FRANCE

Becherel's literary rebrand helped staunch the population decline... and offered an economic lifeline for the future.

Until the eighteenth century, Becherel in Brittany depended economically on its local linen and hemp industry. After this declined it moved into agricultural machinery production, and for a time was home to a successful dairy business. But the beginnings of Becherel's fortuitous journey into book town fame can be traced to the town's inclusion in the national Petites Cités de Caractère project in the late 1970s. The project helped to promote historic rural locations with small populations – in Becherel's case with an emphasis on protecting its Breton culture and heritage.

Becherel officially became France's first book town in 1989, when the Saven Douar cultural association organised the town's first book festival, the Fête du Livre. Since then, it has been followed by seven other French towns which make up the Féderation des Villes, Cités et Villages du Livre en France: Montolieu (1989), Fontenoy-La-Joûte (1996), Cuisery (1999), Charite-sur-Loire (2000), Montmorillon (2000), Ambierle (2007), and Esquelbecq (2007). None are members of the International Organisation of Book Towns.

As with many other book towns, Becherel's literary rebrand helped staunch the population decline – there are now around 800 permanent residents – and offered an economic lifeline for the future.

Today in Becherel there are more than a dozen booksellers and various associated craftspeople offering calligraphy and bookbinding courses. The majority of the books for sale are, unsurprisingly, in French. Among the sellers specialising in titles about Breton history and literature is the Café Librairie Gwrizienn, opened in Becherel's book town infancy by Yvonne Prêteseille. It offers homemade cakes and hot chocolate as well as monthly readings. Its location, Rue de la Chanvrerie, has a previous connection to hemp weaving, and indeed many of the bookshops are situated in attractive buildings that were once the homes and workshops of local fabric merchants.

Above: Bookshops sit side by side on the streets of Becherel.

Right: The quirky sign for bookshop Neiges d'Antan (Snows of Yesteryear), which houses 40,000 books over three floors.

Becherel's bookshops have particularly glorious signs and names – La Vache Qui Lit (The Reading Cow) is a homage to the spreadable French cheese brand La Vache Qui Rit (The Laughing Cow), while Neiges D'Antan (Snows of Yesteryear – 40,000 books over three floors) comes from the famous line in fifteenth-century poet François Villon's *Ballade des dames du temps jadis* – 'Mais où sont les neiges d'antan?'

Other bookshops include:
— Outrepart (Rue Saint-Nicolas) – specialises in parallel literature fiction including utopias, fantasy, and gothic
— La Souris des Champs (Porte Saint-Michel) – sells engravings, old magazines, postcards; has a good stock of cooking and gardening titles
— Librairie du Donjon (Place Alexandre Jehanin) – a varied secondhand stock plus sculptures
— Librairie La Chouette (Place Alexandre Jehanin) – strong on fine illustrated books from the nineteenth and twentieth centuries, and African art
— Bouquinerie Arc-en-Ciel (Rue des Francs Bourgeois) – offers translations services and has a good selection of children's books
— Abraxas-Libris (Rue du Faubourg) – the largest bookshop in Becherel also sells puzzles and board games
— Librairie Yves Grégoire (Place Alexandre Jehanin) – good for history, cinema posters and old copies of *Le Monde* and *Le Figaro*

There are numerous events including an annual book festival at Easter, book markets on the first Sunday of each month, a Nuit du Livre (Book Night) in August, and in March a national poetry event and festival of Ancient Greek and Latin. There are also regular changing exhibitions on book themes in the local Maison du Livre et du Tourisme information centre.

Left: The stock spills out on to the street outside Neiges D'Antan.

Below left: Café Librairie Gwrizienn, where one can browse books over a morning coffee.

Below: On the wall of Café Librairie Gwrizienn stands a quote by René Char – 'Impose ta chance, serre ton bonheur et va vers ton risque. À te regarder, ils s'habitueront', which loosely translates as 'Make your own luck, embrace your happiness and dare to take risks. Watching you, they soon will follow'.

More information

🖙 www.becherel.com

🖙 La Maison du Livre et du Tourisme has a list of bookshop opening times www.becherel.com/cite-du-livre/maison-du-livre-et-du-tourisme

🖙 Becherel is in the Ille-et-Vilaine department. Rennes is the nearest airport, about half an hour away by bus or car. Alternatively, it is a 30km train journey from Combourg and Rennes.

BELLPRAT
CATALONIA, SPAIN

During the town's main festival various houses in the village are temporarily turned into secondhand bookshops.

Bellprat is situated in the beautiful Anoia region of Catalonia.

Bellprat is in many ways the ideal blueprint for a book town. It is set in a beautiful rural location in Catalonia's Anoia region, yet is only ninety minutes away from Barcelona. It has an apppealing unspoilt medieval centre, and its population is – happily for us – enthusiastic about throwing open its doors to book-loving visitors.

It is also the first book town in Catalonia (the second in Spain, after Urueña). A separate project to turn Requena in Valencia into a book town came to an end in 2011 after the local authorities had gone so far as to start restoring a dozen council properties in the old town in readiness to open them as bookshops and printing specialists.

As well as Bellprat, other book towns are being developed in nearby Cervera in Lleida and Montblanc in Tarragona as part of the Viles del Llibre (Book Villages) project to help depressed areas – especially those with abandoned spaces – build a new sustainable economy. So successful have these three been that there are plans to keep the expansion going, opening four more book towns before 2020.

During the town's main festival – which is run during the first weekend in June – various houses in the village are temporarily turned into secondhand bookshops (basements are a popular choice of shop location), along with the many stalls that are set out in a covered market. As well as promoting the village, there is a strong sense of using culture for a good cause – at a recent festival, there was a book swap operation in which books could be exchanged in return for donations to a food bank.

There are also many other book-based events – from conferences, round tables and readings to appearances by dozens of independent regional Spanish publishers. Numerous musical performances and art exhibitions are held throughout the long weekend. At the heart of all the activity is a celebration of Catalan culture (as well as its many literary visitors over the years, controversial Catalan politician Jordi Pujol, former President of the Generalitat of Catalonia, attended the fourth festival), and the town is proud to have elected the first Catalan mayoress, Nativitat Yarza i Planas, in 1934.

Visitors can also stay in the atmospheric Cal Pinyota on Plaza Catalunya, a bookshop-hotel where you can stay in bedrooms with various themes, including the detective novel (with a special nod to the region's most famous fictional detective, Pepe Carvalho), historical fiction, and travel. It also organises creative writing workshops and themed literary weekends for families and children with suggested reading lists, treasure hunts, and craft sessions.

This is very much a community-run book town. From simple beginnings in 2008 when it was set up by the L'Associació d'Amics de Bellprat (Association of Friends of Bellprat), it now offers visitors more than 20,000 books for sale. It's all the more impressive since the population of the village is well under 100.

Sant Jordi

On 23 April, Catalans celebrate their patron saint Sant Jordi in celebrations along similar lines to Valentine's Day – traditionally, women give a red rose to the significant man in their life, while men in return present their wives and girlfriends with a book. In practise, people also include friends and family in the present-giving on the 'dia dels enamorats' ('lovers' day').

Around 8 per cent of all books sold annually in Catalonia (and a third of roses) are sold at this time; roughly 1.5 million paperbacks and hardbacks. In Barcelona, Las Ramblas and Passeig de Gràcia are particularly busy with bookstalls and shoppers. It's also a frantic day for authors, in high demand for book signings.

The Sant Jordi tradition – which happily coincides with Cervantes' and Shakespeare's death dates – inspired UNESCO to name 23 April as World Book Day. Montblanc is among the towns which also holds a reenactment of the famous Jordi and the dragon legend.

Look out for *#BooksAndRoses* on Twitter.

Cervera

Cervera, in the Catalan province of Lleida, also became a book town in 2016, with a festival bringing together thirty publishers and seventy writers at eighty events including storytelling sessions for children, writing jams, and a celebration of the role of the bookmark and bookplate. An emphasis on contemporary Catalan literature is one of the key elements of its future plans. The centre of activities is on Carrer Major, between Plaça Major and Plaça Santa Anna, with the headquarters in the former Wheat Museum. A book market is held here on the first Saturday of each month from 10am to 2pm.

More information

- www.viladelllibre.cat
- Bellprat is around 90km inland from Barcelona by road. The nearest train station is at Igualada, the capital of the Anoia district, 20km to the east.

BORRBY
SWEDEN

'I think that Borrby Bokby is a success... The new bookstores have brought it back to life and we have several families who have moved to Borrby precisely because it is a Bokby.'

Gunnel Ottersten

A street in Sigtuna, which holds a major annual literary festival.

Borrby is in Skåne County in the southernmost part of Sweden with a population of around 1,000. Set up in 2011, one of the organisers' major plans for the Borrby book town, or 'Bokby', is to extend the project to include the surrounding area in what they call a 'Land of Books', with Borrby at the centre. And indeed Skåne boasts the country's largest annual book festival for children and young people, Litteralund, as well as the separate Kristianstad book festival, which is held each autumn. John Steinbeck also dropped in to Borrby on his way to Stockholm to pick up his Nobel Prize for Literature (he bought some paintings).

From the start, plans for the book town were strongly backed by the local chamber of commerce, which was keen to make better use of the town's empty shops, and it received EU grants to help support the plans. During the summer Borrby's lovely sandy beaches make it a popular beach resort, but tourist numbers dwindle considerably outside peak periods.

The plans were spearheaded by secondhand bookshop owner Peter Bodén, who has experience running bookshops in Stockholm, and the project leader is Gunnel Ottersten, who also runs a publishing business in the town.

"I think that Borrby Bokby is a success," says Gunnel. "From being a large and lively village we were heading towards desertification, and shops closed as urbanisation took off and the railway moved many. The new bookstores have brought it back to life and we have several families who have moved to Borrby precisely because it is a Bokby. We are still continuing to develop our version of the book town and plan to hold a major literature festival besides the book days we already have."

As well as various secondhand bookshops (including one specifically for children), galleries and publishers, many of which are gathered in the central Bohuset building, there is also the Språkkafé book café in the old railway station. It runs a special 'language café' every Sunday

afternoon in collaboration with the local refugees support association, to welcome newcomers of all ages and help them learn Swedish. On Tuesdays during the summer, there are also popular writers' meetings at Peter Boden's secondhand Antikvariat Hundörat (The Dog Ear) on Köpmangatan, and monthly weekend book events with speakers, performances and discussion groups.

Sweden's first book town was Mellösa in Södermanland County. About half the size of Borrby and around an hour away from Stockholm (the oldest wheel in Sweden was found there and it is the official county of residence of the Swedish prime minister). Established in 2001, it added a special children's book town in 2009, built to look like Pippi Longstocking's house. Organisers' ill health has meant that it has recently been in abeyance, but there are plans to resurrect it.

Sigtuna Literary Festival

Sigtuna was established in 980, making it Sweden's oldest village. It has around 8,000 residents, the most runic stones of any town in Scandinavia, and the country's oldest surviving written document was found nearby. Since 2012 it has also been home to one of the country's most popular literary festivals.

Although not technically a book town, the organisers hope that it will become Scandinavia's leading literary festival by 2020. It has already grown from a single day to two, with more than

Above: Bokhuset, a meeting place for bookshop and craft enthusiasts.

Right: A plaque proudly celebrates John Steinbeck's visit to Borrby.

eighty events, including a poetry relay on the main square and special events for children. Visiting authors include Samar Yazbek, Anne Enright, Cynthia Haven and Igor Pomerantsev.

Sigtuna is also a member of The International Cities of Refuge Network (ICORN), an independent organisation that offers a home to persecuted writers and artists. Its first guest writer under the scheme was Turkish writer and publisher Ragip Zarakolu, who arrived in 2014.

Above left: A sign outside a bookshop in Sigtuna.

Below left: Inside the Antikvariat Hundörat.

Below: A children's storytelling session taking place during the literary festival.

More information

- www.borrby-bokby.se
- www.litteralund.se/en-gb
- www.turism.kristianstad.se/sv/bokfestivalen
- www.sigtunalitteraturfestival.se
- Borrby is a ninety-minute drive from Malmo. By bus, change at nearby Ystad for the last section of the journey.

BOWRAL
AUSTRALIA

'I felt that the Highlands should be able to support a writers' festival given the number of bookshops, creative people and wineries in the area.'

Michaela Bolzan

The railway station at Bowral.

Bowral, the largest town in the Southern Highlands of New South Wales, was Australia's first book town. With Bong Bong Street as the location for numerous independent bookshops, it opened in 2001 and ran several major festivals, published a Book Trail map to the area (sponsored by HarperCollins, which has a major distribution centre nearby) and ran successful community reading events before hitting problems.

"We ran into some of the issues that have adversely affected other book towns," agrees Paul McShane, who was a driving force in getting the project off the ground and won a Winston Churchill Memorial Trust grant to analyse book towns around the world. "The general problem of rising real estate prices and rents, as well as economic conditions for the book trade, forced the closure of many bookshops in the space of a few years in our region.

"There is still a small core of book town believers here and we continue to look for opportunities to advance the project. The best opportunity that came (and went) was establishing a book town in the historic Berrima Gaol, which would have been a fantastic location. But after decommissioning it and calling for expressions of interest, our State Government has recently started using it as a prison again. This will only be a short-term solution and our time will come again."

Paul is also behind research into Helen Lyndon Goff, one of Bowral's most famous residents, better known as author PL Travers. She created the Mary Poppins character while she was living in the town as a teenager. The town holds the record, set in 2011, for the World's Largest Umbrella Mosaic, formed by 2,115 people.

Happily, into the book town-shaped vaccum stepped Michaela Bolzan, the founder and director of the Southern Highlands Writers' Festival, which has been held in Bowral every July since 2012.

"I felt that the Highlands should be able to support a writers' festival given the number of bookshops, creative people, cafés and wineries in the area," she says. "Because we are an intimate festival of about 1,200 festivalgoers, set in one location, people tell me the SHWF is like the Sydney Writers' Festival was thirty years ago when it first began. A smaller event does allow for more interaction, and I believe a greater exchange of ideas. It remains a passion-project for me. The main reason I continue producing the event is that people love it, and now just expect it to happen!"

Initially, the festival was held over a three-day weekend, but it has now been compacted into one long Saturday and evening in mid-July.

Today there are still several booksellers in Bowral – The Brown Bookshop, The Bookshop Bowral, The Good Reader (all on Bong Bong Street), as well as Dirty Jane's (Banyette Street). Just outside of Bowral are book restoration specialists The Art of Bookbinding and the Berkelouw Book Barn. Situated in the lovely Bendooley Estate, the Book Barn was built at the start of the twentieth century and has recently been restored to expose its timber beams and extraordinarily high ceilings. By day it has a huge stock of new, secondhand, and antiquarian books, and by night it becomes a bookcase-lined event venue, especially popular for wedding receptions.

Above: The Bradman Museum in Bowral.

Below: Members of the audience study the program of events at the Southern Highlands Writers' Festival.

Left: The record-breaking Mary Poppins umbrella mosaic.

Right: A bronze statue of the celebrated literary figure.

More information
- www.mary-poppins-birthplace.net
- www.shwf.com.au
- www.booktown.com.au
- Bowral is a two-hour drive from Canberra and one and a half south-west from Sydney, connected to both by train on the Southern Highlands Line. As well as a regular public bus service, a private charter company offers a direct link to Sydney airport.

BREDEVOORT
NETHERLANDS

Every third Saturday of the month there is a book market in the tree-lined 't Zand Square with bookbinding demonstrations.

Left: A view of Bredevoort showing the town church and windmill.

Bredevoort is in Aalten, Netherlands, close to the border with Germany and in an area of East Guelderland known as De Achterhoek (The Back Corner). It became a book town – Bredevoort Boekenstad – in 2003, and at its height there were around thirty bookshops and book-related businesses. It was a founding member of the International Organisation of Book Towns. Today there are just half of that number and several trade online only.

Local historian and teacher Henk Ruessink was instrumental in getting the book town off the ground, following a major restoration of Bredevoort's medieval centre. Inspired by a trip to Hay-on-Wye, and with the backing of local authorities, he contacted hundreds of booksellers in both Germany and the Netherlands. For those who expressed an interest in taking part, he held a special open day to help sell the concept. The book town won special exemptions from the government to operate on Sundays.

As well as a wide general stock, most of the bookshops also specialise: The English Bookshop (Markt) – history, English literature and illustrated books; Scrinium (Hollendberg) – Greek and Latin classics; The Old Motor Bookshop (Prins Mauritsstraat) – car and tractor books; and Boek en Zo (Landstraat) – mathematics, physics and chemistry, astronomy, medicine and biology. Rainer Heeke, owner of Bücher Mammut (Landstraat, specialising in German books and prints) has also written a book – *Die Praktikantin, le Bookinist & de Boekenstad*. With photographs by Sebastian Hopp, it charts the first twenty years of Bredevoort's experience as a book town. It was published in 2013, the same year he went on a literary pilgrimage by foot to Frankfurt Book Fair to promote the project.

Like Fjærland in Norway (page 53), the town also has numerous honesty bookshops. Among them is the one outside Horus Huiskamertheatertje (Hozenstraat), which claims to be the smallest theatre in the Netherlands (it seats fourteen), and puts on regular shows by storytellers, poets and musicians. Chartae Laudes (Koppelstraat, open on the third Saturday afternoon in the month and by appointment) also provides various book-related services including restoration, bookbinding, and handmade decorative papers.

Every third Saturday of the month there is a book market in the tree-lined 't Zand Square, with bookbinding demonstrations. There is also a tradition of bookfairs in May and August that attract dealers from Germany, Belgium and the Netherlands, and another at Easter for discounted books. A private sellers market is held in July.

Bredevoort also has a thriving *Boekencafé* (book café) run from the town's former Koppelkerk church, now a cultural centre. "It has been transformed into a beacon of art, books and knowledge/understanding," says its director Sylvia Heijnen. "The Bookcafé is a new-style library. With a fireplace, armchairs and a reading table, it is a cosy living room where you can read and buy books. Four booksellers from Bredevoort fill the shelves in different subjects. There are also various literary activities and poetry evenings."

A recent development is the town's Festival van het Papieren Boek (Festival of the Paper Book), a weekend-long summer event including a Nacht van de Poëzie (Night of Poetry), book craft activities and music workshops.

Right: The cobbled streets of the historic city centre.

Below right: Customers eating and reading at the Boekencafé

Opposite above left and opposite below right: There are plenty of bargains to be found at the Bredevoort market.

Below left: The market in full swing in the town square.

Opposite above right: An honesty bookshelf outside an antique bookstore.

More information
- www.festivalvanhetpapierenboek.nl
- www.boekenstad.com
- www.koppelkerk.nl/boekencafe
- Bredevoort is two hours by road from Amsterdam, around an hour and a half from Münster. The nearest railway station is at Aalten, 5km away.

CLUNES
AUSTRALIA

'Clunes reminds me of towns in the Flinders Ranges in South Australia... It has a Wild West quality.'

Alin Golovachenko

A few of the historic buildings so carefully preserved by the inhabitants of Clunes.

Clunes' reinvention as an Australian book town has certainly been dramatic. It was Victoria's first gold rush town and quickly became a major gold producer (one of the bookshops is called The Book Fossicker as a tribute). In some senses little has changed since those days: it retains its rural feel and in 2010 it was awarded the Australian Civic Trust 'Award of Merit' for its 'respectful' use and preservation of heritage buildings. Its unique architectural feel also makes it popular among filmmakers – *Mad Max* starring Mel Gibson was partly filmed here.

Clunes held its first 'Booktown for a Day' event (now known as 'Clunes Booktown Festival') in May 2007. Since then, it has grown to become one of the most successful book towns, proud of its claim to be Australia's largest book trader festival. In 2018 it will be the official host of the biennial Conference of the International Organisation of Book Towns, whose president Tim Nolan chairs Clunes' organising committee.

In addition to its bookshops (even the grocer's and the wine shop sell books), around 18,000 people come to visit its annual festival, which is host to more than fifty book traders, a similar number of author events, exhibitions, and general entertainments from choirs and orchestras to hay bale mazes and medieval Punch and Judy. The cheap $10 weekend pass allows entry to all author talks, entertainment, activities and book stalls, as well as the town's historic buildings. Many of the town's shops become pop-up bookshops for the weekend. On the third Sunday of each month between March and December there are also writer talks in The Warehouse (Fraser Street). All this relies heavily on a small army of volunteers.

"Clunes reminds me of towns in the Flinders Ranges in South Australia," says local photographer Alina Golovachenko, who regularly documents the Booktown Festival. "It has a Wild West quality and doesn't seem over-developed. The first year I shot it for a local visitors' guide

it was cold, book-ish, coffee-ish, people sitting in the street and reading things that they'd just bought, people having long conversations with sellers about particular titles or quietly browsing, a Shakespeare troupe wandering the street…"

A regular visitor to Clunes is The Itty Bitty Book Van. A renovated 1960s caravan, it is a travelling children's bookshop run by Kerri Bennett. Kerri also runs storytelling sessions and other activities including Book Swap events for schools.

The impact of Clunes' book town status has been notable. Its population has doubled in a decade, and it now has a campus for Year 9 students from Wesley College. Its organisers have an international outlook, and the town has a close working relationship with Paju Book City in South Korea (see page 97), collaborating on projects including a celebration of Clunes photographer George Rose, who took historic images of Korea at the start of the twentieth century. It's a success that is being backed by regional grant body Creative Clunes, which has provided substantial investment to keep the good work going.

Readings, Melbourne

Just down the road from Clunes is Melbourne, which not only has numerous flourishing bookshops but is also home to Readings – London Book Fair's International Bookstore of the Year in 2016.

Readings opened in 1969 and is a proudly independent chain – it saw off the arrival of

Above: The entrance to the Bookatorium (open by appointment), run by Robin Schmidt who also owns the online bookshop Huc & Gabet.

Right: Inside the Bookatorium.

Borders across the road – with seven shops around the city including one devoted to children's and young adults' titles. As well as the wide stock, it holds author signings, talks, performances and book launches. Via its charitable arm The Readings Foundation, ten per cent of its profits help to support local literacy and arts projects. Readings has also created an award for new Australian fiction by up-and-coming writers, and another for books.

Far left: Bargain books on sale in Clunes.

Left: Directions pointing visitors in the direction of bookstores.

Below: A young girl peeks through the window of the Itty Bitty Book Van.

More information

- www.clunesbooktown.com.au
- www.readings.com.au
- By road, Clunes is twenty-five minutes from Ballarat and an hour and a half north-west of Melbourne. By train, visitors from Melbourne need to change at nearby Ballarat. A special service runs during festival weekend with extra services each day.

travelling children's bookshop

CUISERY
FRANCE

The impressively bookish gateway into Cuisery.

In her bestselling novel *The Little Paris Bookshop*, Nina George tells the story of Jean Perdu who runs a bookshop/bibliotherapy service from a refurbished barge, and heads off on a journey to Provence. At one point he mentions why he likes Cuisery – which lies on the canalised River Seille, one of France's most popular crusing rivers – so much:

'Oh, Cuisery! An avid reader will lose his heart here. The whole village is crazy about books – or crazy full stop – but that's not unusual. Virtually every shop is a bookshop, a printer's, a bookbinder's, a publisher's, and many of the houses are artists' workshops. The place is buzzing with creativity and imagination.'

The Village du Livre de Cuisery was set up in 1999 as the country's fourth book town, in a bid to counter its declining economy and loss of local shops over the previous decade. At the time there was only one bookshop in the town – there are now fifteen booksellers and book-related professionals. Bookshops were set up in empty premises mostly along the town's main street, Grand Rue, in the medieval area – La Découverte in a former shoe shop, Regards in an old furniture store, L'Espace Gutenberg in a grocery, and Le Livre à Venire in a convenience store. The butcher's was turned into an artist's studio.

Initially there was a full-time worker employed by the Cuisery bookseller's association to manage events, but now they are entirely run by a small army of dedicated volunteers.

Every first Sunday of the month there is a book market which welcomes outside booksellers from around Burgundy, Rhône-Alpes, and Franche-Comté. Other events are organised throughout the year, usually with numerous concerts running simultaneously, including a comic book market in September and poetry readings in springtime.

Printing demonstrations are also available at Espace Gutenberg (Grand Rue) on a copy of the original Gutenberg press (Wednesdays, Thursdays and Saturdays from June to September, and each Saturday from October to May). Bibles and Christian literature are also available in its bookshop. Plans are also in place for a new bookbindery.

Other bookshops specialise in comic books (Charabias, Grand Rue), art (Cuisery Arts, Grand Rue), social and libertarian movements (Les Chats Noirs, Rue du Pavé), speleology and prehistory (La Découverte, Grand Rue), and polar history (Vae Victis, Grand Rue). As Jean Perdu says: "You can find everything here."

The Booksellers' Association is also a small scale publisher. The winners of its annual short story competition are collected in a special booklet, and a special literary heritage tour of the department looks at men and women of letters associated with Cuisery and the surrounding area.

Above: Les Chats Noirs bookshop, which specialises in books on social and libertarian movements.

Right: Books are for sale just about everywhere in Cuisery.

Opposite above left and opposite below left: A few of around fifteen bookstores dotted around Cuisery.

Opposite right: A visitor browses a book stall with Librairie Hérode – publishers of Editions Hérode – pictured in the background.

More information
- www.cuisery-villagedulivre.com
- www.espacegutenberg.com
- www.syndicat-librairie.fr/accueil
- Cuisery is in the Saône-et-Loire department of Burgundy, 110 km north of Lyon and 370 km south of Paris. There are good pontoon moorings for boats at Cuisery.

DAMME
BELGIUM

'Together we run the smallest but finest bookshops of Flanders and the Netherlands.'

Guido De Ville

The canal approach to Damme.

While most book towns are found in attractive locations, visiting Damme in Belgium is a particular treat, as you can cycle the 6km from Bruges along a pretty, flat, tree-lined path alongside the River Reie, which has now been canalised (Damme was Bruges's port in the thirteenth century).

Damme has been a book town since 1997 and has nine bookshops. Although times vary, they are generally open daily between May and September, then at weekends over the winter. There is also a book market on the Market Square every second Sunday in the month, from 10am to 5pm (held inside the Town Hall during the winter). The market has a theme each month (for example travel, poetry or romance), and at least a quarter of each stall's titles must be related to the subject.

"We accumulated a couple of old guide books, a paperback of US sea shanties and a Johnny Weissmuller/Tarzan film poster at the weekly book market," says Sarah Henshaw, who runs floating bookshop The Book Barge, which has travelled the length of Britain's waterways and since relocated to France. She has visited Damme several times. "The Weissmuller purchase, really, was an act of mercy, it being incongruously sandwiched between thirty or so other 'movie' posters of a less wholesome, Nazi porno bent."

Many of the bookshops can be found thanks to their traditional metal signs, complete with unique Damme book town branding – one of the many indicators of this town's passionate community spirit. Among the pick of the bookshops is Oorlog en Vrede (War and Peace) on Burgstraat – which calls itself 'the loneliest bookshop in town'. Postcards, comics and maps share shelf space with a healthly secondhand stock, a decent English language section, and multiple volumes on both World Wars. Willy Tibergien and Guido De Ville

Above: All manner of books for sale in Damme town square.

Right and above right: Signs direct visitors to Oorlog & Vrede (War & Peace), the 'loneliest bookshop' in Damme.

Far right: A secondhand book market takes place on a summer weekend in Damme.

proudly manage Feniks (Phoenix) which covers just 15 square metres. "Together we run the smallest but finest bookshop of Flanders and the Netherlands in the town hall," says Guido. The shop stocks poetry, both in Dutch and English, as well as local history, art and novels. Other bookshops include Boekhandel Ballade, (Kerkstraat) – travel guides, art, cookbooks; D'Oede Schole (Burgstraat) – African history; Antiquariaat Maerlant (Burgstraat) – literary history, Belgian Congo; and Boeken Diogenes (Kerkstraat) – local history, antiques.

Among its other literary claims to fame, Damme is said to be the 'birthplace' of fictional trickster/folk hero Till Eulenspiegel. The town has a whole museum dedicated to him and the various versions of his roguish story through the centuries. It was also the home of Jacob van Maerlant, one of the most important Dutch poets in the Middle Ages (his statue can be found close to Feniks).

More information
- www.visitdamme.be/en
- Damme is easily accessible from Bruges by bicycle (which can be rented from one of the numerous bike shops in Bruges and from some hotels), canal boat or public bus. By car, the journey takes around ten minutes.

Tables laden with books encourage shoppers into Feniks bookshop.

FEATHERSTON
NEW ZEALAND

While Featherston is a book town in its own right, it is also a central hub for literary activities in the surrounding Wairarapa area.

The dramatic approach to Featherston.

Featherston is one of the newest book towns, becoming a member of the International Organisation of Book Towns in 2015.

Inspired by the success of Clunes in Australia, its main event is an annual weekend-long book fair in May which attracts antiquarian and secondhand booksellers from all over New Zealand and Australia. Their stalls are largely set up in the ANZAC Hall, on the corner of Birdwood and Bell Streets, built a century ago to provide entertainment for soldiers based in the town's enormous Military Training Camp.

During the fair the whole town gets into the spirit with themed window displays, murals, and art installations. Other events include an *Antiques Roadshow*-style Antiquarian Book Consultation, improvised theatre workshops based on popular children's literature, bookbinding and other papercraft workshops.

"When the founding group first approached locals about the concept of book towns, faces were blank, if not frozen. Even after explanations about other towns, and how they've achieved regeneration, disbelief was rampant," admits Featherston's Operations Manager Kate Mead, who runs the town's Loco bookshop-café (Fitzherbert Street).

"I now believe in the aphorism 'success breeds success'. Before our first book town events, I talked endlessly to local businesses about the concept of book towns, and specifically about decorating their windows with book-related themes. Our book town art group worked so hard, making gorgeous decorations and then taking them around and physically putting them up in business premises. Year Two, and we had business owners asking, sometimes impatiently, about when their windows would be festooned with bookish loveliness. It was a similar story with media, who prevaricated about, or outright declined, giving us column space, let alone editorial at the outset, but who are now onboard

Above: St John's Anglican Church in Featherston provides an atmospheric location for bookselling.

Right: The aim of the book town is to improve the local quality of life.

and asking for meetings to work out how they can help promote our next events."

As well as Featherston's own bookshops including the family-run For The Love of Books (Fitzherbert Street), there is also Almo's Books in nearby Carterton, and Writer's Plot, Readers Read in Upper Hutt, half an hour away by train. This bookshop is a not-for-profit incorporated society run by volunteers which specialises in New Zealand authors and medium and small press books. It also provides workspace for writers and runs its own writer in residence programme.

But while Featherston (population: 2,500) is a book town in its own right, it is also a central hub for literary activities in the surrounding Wairarapa area. One of the most popular ongoing events is the Yarns in Barns biennial literary festival, first held in 2003, co-founded by Hedley's Booksellers which is based in the region's largest town of Masterton around 35km from Featherston. Events (including the headline event held in a woolshed) take place all round the area including in Gladstone. Similarly, the Wairarapa Poetry on the Highway project in 2014 linked more than sixty shops along the State Highway 2 in Featherston, Greyton, Carterton and Masterton, with favourite poems on display in businesses' windows.

"We have three excellent primary schools in town and one of Featherston book town's generous benefactors is going to offer a $10 voucher to every child at our schools to spend over the festival weekend," says Kate. "For some of these children it will be their first book purchase, ever. It will encourage their families to attend book town events, most of which are free, or admission by Koha/donation. Our ambition for Featherston book town is to establish an identity that subtly, but directly, improves the quality of life for everyone who lives here."

Wellington Writers' Walk

Not far down the road from Featherston is Wellington, which has a wide range of bookshops and its own literary happenings. Among these is the Writers' Walk along the city's waterfront. Arranged in concrete plaques and large metal letters are twenty-three quotations from some of the country's finest writers with a connection with Wellington, including Katherine Mansfield and New Zealand Maori author Patricia Grace. A free trail booklet is available from Wellington libraries and tourist information centres.

More information

- www.booktown.org.nz
- www.wellingtonwriterswalk.co.nz
- Featherston is just over an hour's very scenic drive from Wellington on the State Highway 2, or slightly less by train (special bicycle carriages are available). The Rimutaka Cycle Trail links Featherston to Wellington through lovely scenery.

Above: Featherston particularly encourages younger readers.

Below: On the Wellington Writers' Walk is a plaque displaying a quote from Dennis Glover's poem 'Wellington Harbour is a Laundry'.

FJÆRLAND
NORWAY

Fjærland is home to a dozen new and secondhand bookshops in various hotels and rural buildings, including old sheds, ferry buildings and even a former pigpen.

Fjærland (population: 300, but with up to 300,000 tourists a year), known as Den Norske Bokbyen (The Norwegian Book Town), is the most dramatically picturesque book town in the world. Located by the Sognefjord next to mainland Europe's largest glacier, Jostedalsbreen, it has long been popular with tourists, but until the end of the last century it could be reached only by boat. A series of road tunnels through the mountains, opened in the 1980s and 1990s, made the village more accessible.

Fjærland is home to a dozen new and secondhand bookshops in various hotels and rural buildings, including old sheds, ferry buildings, and even a former pigpen. A guiding principle of the book town is that old structures should be reused sensitively. Books are also available in art galleries, shops, hotels and naturally the book café Kaffistova. In addition, there are various honesty *Sjølvplukk* (bookshops) by the sides of the road. In total, there are around three miles of shelving.

Established in 1995, most of the books sold in the book town are in Norwegian, but there are plenty in English too with several shops specialising in certain areas. Arnold, in a former boathouse and stables, concentrates on historical and contemporary titles, while Gamle-Posten (the Old Post Office) offers fiction, comics, and books in English. Odin, at the ferry waiting area, focuses on literary fiction and poetry. Tusund Og Ei Natt (Thousand and One Nights), claims to have the largest stock of religious literature in the country as well as a good English language section, and Bok og bilde (Books & Pictures) also sells records. Overall, the largest secondhand bookshop is Straumsvågs Antikvariat. The town also distributes publications from Sjørettsfondet, the Norwegian Maritime Law Foundation.

The main bookselling season runs from May to late September and the bookshops are usually open daily from 10am to 6pm, although one or two places do carry on into winter (which gets pretty nippy, temperatures plummeting to -20°C). The historic Hotel Mundal, a strong supporter of the book town, is a good place to stay and is a key location in the novel *The Castle in the Pyrenees* by Jostein Gaarder, author of *Sophie's World*. Fjaerland also features prominently in his bestselling children's book, co-authored with Klaus Hagerup, *Bibbi Bokken's Magiske Bibliotek* (*Bibbi Bokken's Magic Library* – available in numerous translations but not yet in English).

The town also holds book-related events during the main opening period, in particular its weekend 'Boknatti', the annual Solstice Bookfair. The intriguing concept behind its success is that you hire a stand (which comes with a free table and chair) and sell your own secondhand books long into the night. The book fair features readings, talks, author interviews and concerts, and finishes at around 2am on Sunday morning.

In addition to welcoming customers, the town is also keen to encourage volunteers to work in its bookshops over the summer, and runs a popular membership scheme. By signing up to be a 'Friend of The Norweigan Booktown' (send an email to post@bokbyen.no) you receive a 10 per cent discount off all secondhand books, as well as discounts on accommodation and activities in the area.

Perhaps the best view from a bookshop in the world.

Left: A book-filled bedroom in the Fjærland Hotel.

Above right: An honesty bookshop on the side of the road, on the shores of Sognefjord.

Below right: Shopping for books during book night.

More information

🕮 bokbyen.no

🕮 A passenger boat runs between Mundal/ Fjærland and Balestrand in the summer, and also links up with buses leaving for the glaciers on a daily basis. Fjærland is a six hour drive from Oslo and there are buses each day to nearby towns including Sogndal (thirty minutes) where there is an airport.

FONTENOY-LA-JOÛTE
FRANCE

At its height there were twenty-three booksellers in the village. Its first book fair in September 1994 attracted around 11,000 visitors.

Before Fontenoy-la-Joûte was set up as a book town it had no connection with the literary world at all, and indeed very few businesses of any kind before the Les Amis du Livre association was established in 1994. The book town was officially inaugurated two years later, thanks to the efforts of a small band of enthusiasts, including France's former Minister of Agriculture, François Guillaume, and the village's mayor Jean-Marie Vanot.

A total of eighteen businesses opened their doors in April 1996, with bookshops planning to open at weekends and holidays, and more frequently during the summer. Within four years the project had created thirty-seven jobs, and two-dozen buildings had been renovated for new use. At its height there were twenty-three booksellers in the village. Its first book fair in September 1994 attracted around 11,000 visitors, and booksellers from France, Belgium and Luxembourg. These monthly fairs helped the town to draw nearly 100,000 visitors a year.

These numbers have fallen, but there are still ten bookshops and a calligraphy studio – L'encre et l'Image on Rue Saint-Pierre – and Fontenoy attracts peripatetic art festivals such as Apprentiss'ART, which in 2016 put on a display of literary origami. An annual writing contest has also been held for the last two decades, with the winning entries published in a short book.

An interesting landmark is the unusual signpost in the village centre. As well as pointing to other book towns around the world it features imaginary locations including Atlantis, and Edgar Rice Burrough's fictitious 'hollow earth', Pellucidar.

The oldest bookshop in Fontenoy is the marvellously-named A la recherche du Livre Perdu (Rue Saint-Pierre). Also dating back to 1996 is Le Chat Botté (Rue Division Leclerc) with its huge arched doorway and natural stone wall interiors. L'Etable (Rue Saint-Pierre) specialises in *bandes dessinées* (comic books), while Paragraphes and Nuit de Chine (both on Rue Division Leclerc) are

good for children's books. La Forge 54 (Rue du Paquis) concentrates on architecture and esoteric subjects; Librairie Viollet (Rue Division Leclerc) on history and posters. La Porte Retrouvée (Rue Saint-Pierre), formerly N'en faites pas un roman (Don't write a novel about it), is strong on science fiction and also has a good selection of vinyl records.

Chinguetti

One of the arrows on the village's curious signpost points to a very distant, unexpected location: 'Chinguetti, La Sorbonne du désert – Mauritanie, 3506 km'. This former trading post in Mauritania was twinned with Fontenoy as part of the village's tenth anniversary celebrations. Rather than a *village du livre*, Chinguetti is more of a *cité des lettres*. It has been home to numerous libraries for hundreds of years, many run as family affairs. These hold a particularly impressive collection of scientific and Koranic texts, and as a result UNESCO has awarded it World Heritage Site status.

More information

👉 www.villagedulivre54.fr
👉 Fontenoy-la-Joûte is in eastern France in the Meurthe-et-Moselle département, 55km south-east of Nancy and an hour and a half from Strasbourg by car. Free parking is plentiful throughout the village, and there is a dedicated area for RVs. The nearest train station is Baccarat, 10km away, with a shuttle bus link service.

Opposite: The famous sign pointing towards book towns and beyond.

Left: A family librarian at work in Chinguetti.

Above: Books of every genre are available at this secondhand bookshop, from comics and novels to craft books.

GOLD CITIES
CALIFORNIA, USA

'Plenty of collectors come in looking for something special. One never knows what one might find if one looks hard enough.'

Karen Wright

The twin book cities of Grass Valley and Nevada City sit on the edge of Tahoe National Forest, California.

The Gold Cities Book Town in California was inspired by a trip to Hay-on-Wye and set up in 1997 largely thanks to the efforts of local bookmen Gary Stollery and John Hardy. It actually covered two main locations, Grass Valley and (four miles to the north) Nevada City, with satellite sellers in nearby Penn Valley, North San Juan, and Lake of the Pines. Richard Booth himself attended the book town's foundation, and at its peak it had more than thirty bookshops. Unfortunately, despite this promising start and the launch of an annual Gold Rush Book Fair, bookshop numbers have been in decline. The huge Ames Bookstore closed in 2016 and the official Gold Cities Book Town organisation has fallen by the wayside.

However, in Nevada City, Gary Stollery still runs a bookshop, Toad Hall Books (N Pine Street), with his wife Clarinda. Hardy Books, open by appointment only, still specialises in Western Americana and 'All Things Californian', much of which is not included in its online inventory. Mountain House Books (online only) holds a general stock, especially strong on California Gold Rush titles as well as prints from the seventeenth to the nineteenth centuries.

Meanwhile, Jenny's Paper & Ink Books (Joerschke Drive) offers preowned delights in Grass Valley, which is also home to Booktown Books, a co-operative venture established by a group of book dealers in 1998. The project has gradually expanded, and since 2005 has operated from a two-story, 4,000 square foot building. Each bookseller has their own booth space and displays their chosen genres of books – military history, esoteric, graphic novels, or simply general - as well as book ephemera, DVDs, CDs and vinyl records. Bud Plant and Hutchison Books, for example, specialises in fine illustrated and children's books in Booths 8 and 10, and Main Street Antiques & Books has a booth as well as a shop in Nevada City.

"The building which houses this bookopolis was built in the 1930s to serve as a Salvation Army regional office, and later it had many other incarnations until Booktown Books showed it its true destiny," explains booth-holder Karen Wright, owner of The Wright Book. "It has been very nicely restored and adapted with a big, open space with high ceilings and lots of windows. The location is fabulous, right in the heart of the historic Old Town Grass Valley which dates from the early 1850s.

"We took the upstairs balcony for classics and modern fiction and nonfiction in many subjects. Upstairs might not have been the best space because it is rather remote and people are sometimes too lazy to climb, however, with some creative advertising it works. The best part of a co-op is that we have a bookstore and only have to be there part of the time."

Every book is coded and priced by each bookseller in Booktown Books. This means you could find half a dozen copies of a book in six different booths at six different prices. There is one communal display case and one glass case downstairs in the main room with plenty of shelves where dealers rotate their displays monthly. There are also several spinner racks and a table in front where special books are on offer. A recent innovation is the rare 'book room' in Booth 16, but the general overall stock is in the mid- to low- price range with occasional sales going on in different booths.

"It is kind of a pain to keep track of who has what sale at any particular moment," admits Karen, "but it works out. The most popular books are the new best sellers and classics, but plenty of collectors come in looking for something special. One never knows what one might find if one looks hard enough. Many people bring in books to sell. Whichever dealers are on the desk on any given day, have first choice of books that come in the door."

Each dealer works a required number of hours a month based on how much space they have, while rents are calculated on occupied space – booths are all different sizes and if one dealer wants more than one booth, then they will pay the rent on that additional space. "Who gets what newly opened space is determined by seniority, or occasionally a new bookseller comes along looking for a space," explains Karen, who specialises in sci-fi, fantasy, and supernatural fiction, as well as occult and Native Americana. "If a booth is empty, it is not good as the rest of the dealers have to split the rent on that space to pay the landlord until the space is filled, but that doesn't happen too often.

"We don't have a boss, we make decisions by vote at meetings. One of the dealers has taken on the responsibility of the rather archaic bookkeeping system for the rest of us and there are other jobs each of us picks up when they need doing, such as changing displays when a dealer is not there at rotation time, and making the signs and posters for events, fixing the electrical system, or blowing the leaves off the porches in the fall."

Interestingly, Booktown is not the only book operation run on these lines in the area. The Open Book in Grass Valley was established in 1994, originally as Tomes Bookstore. But since 2015 it has been run along collective lines with volunteers working regular three-hour shifts and organising evening events. Volunteer privileges include unlimited book borrowing. The Open Book is also home to independent book publisher The Open Book Press.

More information

📖 Booktown Books (booktownbooks.com), 107 Bank Street, Grass Valley, California. Open Monday to Saturday, 10am-6pm, Sunday 11am-5pm.

📖 Grass Valley and Nevada City are just over an hour's drive from Sacramento and its international airport, and two and a half hours from San Francisco.

Right: Inside the impressive Booktown Books, a cooperative bookselling space housed in an old Salvation Army regional office, which covers two storeys and 4,000 square feet.

Below left: Main Street in the old gold mining town of Grass Valley.

Below middle: The shopfronts of downtown Nevada City.

Below right: Historic Nevada City in fresh snow.

HAY-ON-WYE
WALES

'Hay changed from a small market town into a mecca for secondhand book lovers.'

Roger Williams

Book stalls in the grounds of Hay Castle.

Hay-on-Wye (Y Gelli Gandryll) is where the book town was born. The concept was the brainchild of bookseller Richard Booth, who in 1977 crowned himself the King of Hay and announced that his home town was an independent kingdom (he later established a Hay House of Lords with its own hereditary peers). Behind this headline-grabbing showmanship was a serious message, that local economies need support to survive and prevent the drain of talented locals to cities. Crucially too, he saw this as an international project, planning and developing sustainable book towns around the world who would work together in a semi-formal network. Indeed, Hay is twinned with the book town of Redu in Belgium (see page 107).

Booth opened his first bookshop in 1961 in Hay's former fire station and built up his stock by shipping books over from New York. Others followed throughout the 1970s and Hay became known as a town of books. By any count it has been a success – numerous non-bookish businesses as well as related ones such as bookbinders have also successfully established themselves here – and Booth's part in it was rewarded with an MBE in 2004. According to local MP Roger Williams: "His legacy will be that Hay changed from a small market town into a mecca for secondhand book lovers, and this transformed the local economy." His The King of Hay Bookshop on Castle Street sells ephemera related to his success as well as a varied secondhand and antiquarian stock of books.

A major spin-off from Booth's success is that the town is also host in late May and early June to the annual 10-day Hay Literary Festival (which itself has spawned sister 'Hay' festivals around the world in Mexico, Spain, Colombia, Denmark, and Peru). Established by Peter Florence in 1988, it attracts hundreds of thousands of international visitors and major literary, scientific, musical and political figures every year. It has been joined more recently by a new philosophy and music festival, How The Light Gets In.

There are many secondhand booksellers in Hay – indeed, during the festival the Hay History Group runs a special bookshop tour - although perhaps the best known is the rejuvenated outdoor Honesty Bookshop at Hay Castle which has been selling books for £1 or less since the 1960s, proceeds going towards the ongoing restoration of the castle as a cultural and heritage centre. The largest is the enormous Richard Booth's Bookshop (Lion Street), now run by Elizabeth Haycox and also home to a 47-seat cinema, café and studio space, as well as serving as an occasional wedding venue. Addyman Books is a small empire of bookshops in the town which started in a small room at the Blue Boar Inn and now takes in Murder and Mayhem (Lion Street, focusing on detective fiction – look out for the atmospheric chalk body outline on the floor...) and Addyman Annexe (Castle Street, specialising in what it describes as 'sexier material: beat, sex, drugs, art, modern firsts, poetry, philosophy, left wing history and the occasional occult work').

Other bookshops include:

— C. Arden (Forest Road) – natural history, gardening, ornithology and beekeeping
— Hay Cinema Bookshop (Castle Street) – the former picture house became a bookshop in 1965 and claims to have the world's largest open-air bookshop (not to mention 200,000 volumes indoors) as well as providing books

as props for shops, film sets and plays. Its top floor is also home to Francis Edwards which has a good antiquarian stock and a branch in London's Charing Cross.
— Mostlymaps (Castle Street) – antique maps
— The Childrens Bookshop (Newport Street) – children's titles with an emphasis on twentieth-century fiction. Also good for children's and illustrated books is Rose's Books (Broad Street)
— Hancock & Monks Music (Broad Street) – has sold recorded and printed classical music for forty years
— Poetry Bookshop (Brook Street) – the only 100% secondhand poetry bookshop in the UK
— Boz Books (Castle Street) – emphasis on nineteenth century English Literature and an especially wide selection of Charles Dickens titles

In addition, the labyrinthine Broad Street Book Centre is an umbrella operation with 15 booksellers under one roof offering a very wide selection (there is a similar operation in Grass Valley, California, see page 61) and a particularly impressive stock of railway-related books. There are also usually secondhand books on sale at the well-attended weekly Thursday Market around the town.

Bizarrely, considering its book heritage, in recent years the town has been fighting to avoid the closure of its library, a campaign supported by the organisers of the Hay Festival.

Opposite: A key book town landmark, Richard Booth's Bookshop.

Below: Booksellers flourish on High Town Street.

Bottom: Addyman Books is a reading-only zone.

Right: Murder and Mayhem, Hay-on-Wye's crime specialist.

Right below: A mother and son enjoy the fruits of the annual Hay literary festival, held over ten days and featuring talks and appearances by some of the world's most treasured authors.

The Story of Books

The newest bookish addition to the book town is The Story of Books museum, set up by Emma Balch at the appropriately-named Baskerville Hall hotel in Clyro, just outside the main town. It is set to be the UK's first museum entirely dedicated to the printed word, and will feature working vintage printing presses, temporary exhibitions (the first two focused on illustrated books and book production) and many hands-on workshops including papermaking, marbling and printmaking. As well as using the vintage equipment to run a publishing company, there will also be digital and interactive elements. The whole enterprise is a listed B-Corp – the equivalent of a Fair Trade certification – with a strong emphasis on ethical and community values. Promoting the Welsh language and providing employment for local residents will be among its main priorities.

More information
- www.hay-on-wye.co.uk
- www.hayfestival.com
- www.thestoryofbooks.com
- Hay-on-Wye is around 50 miles from Worcester and 60 miles from Cardiff by road. The nearest train stations are in Hereford and Builth Wells, a request stop. Bristol International Airport is 80 miles away.

Opposite: Hay is a favourite wedding venue for literary types, and suitably picturesque.

Above: Baskerville Hall, home of The Story of Books museum.

Left: Looking towards Hay from the Offa's Dyke Path, a popular route for ramblers.

HOBART
NEW YORK, USA

Don Dales decided that the many empty shops could provide the raw ingredients to make a thriving book town.

One of the smallest bookshops to be found in any book town.

In the same way that Richard Booth drove the success of Hay, Hobart Book Village owes a huge debt to one man. The small town of around 400 residents, in a picturesque rural location in the northern Catskills, now has six bookshops all very close to each other on Main Street, and was awarded the Delaware County Chamber of Commerce Tourism Award in 2016. This is all thanks to musician Don Dales, who in 1999 decided that the many empty shops at the time could provide the raw ingredients to make a thriving book town.

He bought up various premises and offered them to new businesses on tiny rents, sometimes even for free. He was soon joined by Diana and Bill Adams, who run WM. H. Adams Antiquarian Bookshop, specialising in pre-nineteenth-century and classical titles. It spreads over three floors and has an attractive deck overlooking the Delaware river. The bookshop is also the venue for the annual Winter Respite Lecture Series (check the Hobart Book Village website for details). Don now runs the Mysteries & More Crime Café in a Greek Revival house dating back to the 1830s with a good stock of mystery, detective and science fiction titles as well as homemade snacks.

The newest arrival is Kathy and George Duyer's Creative Corner Books, which concentrates on cookery and craft books but also organises cookery demonstrations, knitting clinics, and workshops on the premises, as well as stocking locally-produced farm products.

A good example of how things have changed is Liberty Rock Books, which was built in the eary 1920s and was formerly an auto garage and propane distributor. Now the 5,000-square-foot space with exposed beams is full of books, including Native American works, plus jazz records and CDs, and vintage postcards. Other bookshops include Butternut Valley Books, which stocks a good range of local and global

Left: Former auto garage and propane dispenser, Liberty Rock Books.

Below left: The exterior of WM. H. Adams Antiquarian Books.

Below: A bookstore beckons customers.

maps, fine art prints and bookends, as well as books in a variety of languages. The book village also hosts large book sales on Memorial Day and Thanksgiving Day, as well as an annual short story competition.

Every September, Hobart is the venue for the Hobart Festival of Women Writers. Set up in 2013 by Barbara Balliet and Cheryl Clarke, it includes flash reading events, writing workshops, play readings and author appearances. Barbara and Cheryl also run Blenheim Hill Books, which focuses on women's studies, poetry, African American literature, and children's books.

In addition to the bookshops, Paper Moon Bookbinding sells a wide range of bookish ephemera, produces its own handmade cards, and repairs books.

Right: The impressive façade at Mysteries & More, safely guarded by shop cat Big Red below.

More information
- www.hobartbookvillage.com
- www.hobartfestivalofwomenwriters.com
- Hobart is in Delaware County, New York state, on Route 10, around three hours from New York City (Brooklyn) by car.

LA CHARITÉ-SUR-LOIRE

FRANCE

At its peak the town had around fifteen booksellers, with some intriguing names including Le monde a l'envers (The upside down world).

Looking along the river towards La Charité-sur-Loire.

La Charité-sur-Loire, in the Nièvre department of Burgundy in central France, became a *villes du livre* in 2000. It was established when an exodus of Parisian booksellers, led by rare book specialist Christian Valleriaux, looking for less expensive premises (and homes) headed south. At its peak the town had around fifteen booksellers, with some intriguing names including Le monde a l'envers (The upside down world), La, ou dort le chat (There, where the cat sleeps), and Les palmiers sauvages (The Wild Palms). The heaviest concentration of bookshops has traditionally been in the lower part of town, home to around 5,500 permanent residents.

Although the number of bookshops has fallen, there remains an ongoing commitment to the world of books via two main organisations: Les Amis de la Ville du Livre and Les Petits Salons. Between them they organise major book fairs in July and August (when traffic is restricted for Nuit du livre events and late opening hours) and

book markets from October to March on the third Sunday of the month. These are usually organised around a theme and held indoors in the priory.

One of the central locations for the book town is its UNESCO World Heritage Site, the priory of Notre-Dame de la Charité-sur-Loire, which dates back to the eleventh century. Following major restoration works it is now a cultural centre as well as a stopping point along the Santiago de Compostella pilgrimage route. It runs a year-long programme of lectures, exhibitions, seminars and other book-related events. There are also various book craft specialists in La Charité-sur-Loire including Callibris, run by Patricia Muller, which concentrates on calligraphy and illumination.

The town's Festival du Mot has been held at the end of each May since 2005. It is a general celebration of words in theatre, dance, music and the visual arts as well as, naturally, in books. Every year a jury of writers and language experts, with help from a public vote, chooses 'the word of

the year'. Winners include 'refugees' (2016), 'selfie' (2014) and 'bling-bling' (2008).

There is also the Balade des Mots literary walking trail, which encourages visitors to wander the streets and note the various famous quotations from writers including Kipling, Guy De Maupassant and Victor Hugo (there are also Chinese, Sufi and Japanese proverbs) that have been painted on the outside walls of shops and houses (the Danish book town Ingstrup has run a similar project). Among them is 'Ce que l'on conçoit bien s'énonce clairement, et les mots pour le dire arrivent aisément' ('What is conceived well is expressed clearly, and the words to say it come easily') by seventeenth-century poet and critic Nicolas Boileau and 'La pensée vole et les mots vont à pied. Voilà tout le drame de l'écrivain' (Thoughts fly and words travel on foot. Therein lies the drama of writing') by author Julien Green.

Left: The upside down bookshop.

Above right: Librarie Gilles Hamm, specialists in *bandes dessinées* (comic books) and manga comics.

Below right: The words of famous writers are written on the book town's walls as part of the literary walking trail.

More information
- 🐭 www.festivaldumot.fr
- 🐭 www.citedumot.eu
- 🐭 www.lacharitesurloire-tourisme.com/ ville-du-livre
- 🐭 Paris is two hours away by car, Auxerre just over an hour, and by direct train.

LANGENBERG
& KATLENBURG
GERMANY

A 500-year-old town full of half-timbered buildings with cobblestone streets and encircled by ancient woodland, Langenberg is popular with visitors from nearby Düsseldorf and Cologne.

Pastor Martin Weskott posing for a photo in his office. For nearly 20 years, Reverend Martin Weskott has been saving books printed in the former East Germany from the rubbish heap of history.

Bücherstadt Langenberg was founded in 1998 and is run by fifty members of a dedicated non-profit organisation. It currently has regular book markets, half a dozen secondhand bookshops, a permanent exhibition of early Dante editions, and two art galleries including Ananda run by Elmar Lamers. Ananda also sells old travel guides (especially Baedekers from 1880 to 1945), vintage photo prints, engravings, maps and miniature books.

Bookbinder and restorer Michael Rönsberg regularly opens his workshop on Hauptstraße to the public, while Der Gutenberg – Die Buchmacherey (Mühlenstraße), run by Hans Josef Altmann, features two printing presses from the time of Gutenberg. As well as running printing workshops, he also takes them on the road for school visits and medieval markets.

It's certainly a very atmospheric location. A 500-year-old town full of half-timbered buildings with cobblestone streets and encircled by ancient woodland, Langenberg is popular with visitors from nearby Düsseldorf and Cologne, both just an hour's drive away. It's also a historic town, once home to one of the country's largest paper factories and a popular spot among the great and the good of pre-First World War Prussia.

Katlenburg

The Johannes-Kirchengemeinde in Katlenburg, three hours' drive east of Langenburg, is a remarkable one-man book church. As the Berlin Wall was falling in 1991, Pastor Martin Weskott noticed that thousands of unwanted but entirely readable books from East German libraries and publishers were being thrown into landfill in Leipzig. Outraged, Weskott borrowed a truck and made dozens of trips to salvage as many as he could, bringing them back to his Lutheran church in Katlenburg where he stored them in a neighbouring barn.

Since then, he has continued to collect and then give books away free to parishioners – and indeed all visitors – after Sunday services with donations passed on to charities. Over the years, Pastor Weskott and his team of a dozen volunteer helpers have saved more than one million books of all genres, from foreign literature to medical text books. Many have also been sent abroad to worthy causes. He stores a similar number on the church's premises.

Above: Printer Hans Josef Altmann in his printing shop.

Above right: Bücherhaus – a bookshop, café and bakery all rolled into one.

Right: Inside the Bücherhaus.

More information
🖝 www.buecherstadt-langenberg.de
🖝 www.buecherburg.de
📖 Langenberg is a twenty minute drive from Essen and half an hour by train from Wuppertal and Essen.

Far left: The dramatic Bürgerhaus in Langenburg, which serves as the centre of the town's administration.

Above left: The Tourist Information office is also the book town's headquarters.

Below left: The charming façades of Langenburg's old town.

LILLEPUTHAMMER
NORWAY

The main section is a miniature copy of the main street in the city of Lillehammer, Storgata, with all the houses built at quarter size.

A bird's eye view of Lilleputhammer.

All book towns sell children's books, and some booksellers focus entirely on young people's titles. There is even the Hall of Kembuchi (also known as the Children's Picture Book Museum) an enormous library-museum-exhibition centre in the Japanese village of Hokkaido with a stock of more than 60,000 illustrated books and its own children's book awards. But there is only one children's book town – Lilleputhammer in Norway.

Lilleputthammer is a small adventure park for children and their families. The main section is a miniature copy of the main street in the city of Lillehammer, Storgata, with all the houses built as they looked in the 1930s but at quarter size. In total there are more than forty shops, two hotels, three cafés, two bakeries, a police station and a cinema. Many of these are still running. Within this is the Children's City of Books; six houses in the street devoted entirely to books.

"We have about 15,000 books in different genres, all made for children," explains Cathrine Wilhelmsen, Deputy General Manager. "The books are divided into different houses according to the ages of the readers and then again into different categories such as animals, fairytales, environmental protection, cowboys, crime, nature and outdoors living. The houses are When Mum and Dad Were Young (books written between 1900 and 1970), Picture Book House, Youth-literature, Mysteries and Crime, The Comics House, and The House of Facts. In addition we also have a bookshop with newly published books, stationary, nostalgic art and fun stuff."

All the books are secondhand, either donated from local libraries or sent in by the public. There is also a shop selling contemporary Norwegian children's literature. There are frequent readings and short plays, and if concentration begins to wane – the park is aimed at children under ten – there is also a small train, a rollercoaster, and trampolines, as well as craft activities.

Biblo Tøyen: Children-only library

Biblo Tøyen is a library in Oslo for everybody – so long as they are between ten and fifteen years old. Adults are not allowed in and must wait outside for their offspring to emerge. The library is run along normal lines using special library cards for borrowing books, and caters particularly for children after the school day is over, but its architecture is not so traditional. After consulting young readers in focus groups, the designers have installed a Volvo truck with a functional kitchen in the back (the library also runs various activities including cookery courses) and a reading sofa in the bonnet. Library users can also enjoy their books in a ski-lift gondola hanging from the ceiling, a converted tuk-tuk, barber's chair, or numerous wheelbarrows.

In keeping with this approach, there is nothing Dewey Decimal about the library's classification system; books are instead arranged by themes such as 'short' or 'animals'. This also means that no book has a fixed location. At night, a dedicated book drone flies around the library to scan and update the books' positions.

Above: An unbeatable mixture of books and merry-go-rounds.

Right: Children relax with books in the summer sunshine, nestled among the miniature houses.

Right: Bookshops are built for younger readers, so adults best mind their heads!

Below left: A reading session takes place in one of the book houses.

Below right: The Biblo Tøyen in Oslo.

More information

☞ www.lilleputthammer.no

☞ Kenbuchi-ehon-yakata.com

☞ Lilleputthammer is in Hafjell, 15km north of Lillehammer, around twenty minutes by car and with regular bus connections.

MONTEREGGIO
ITALY

As the number and weight of the books increased, the sellers turned to using carts pulled by hand or by horses.

The rolling hills and winding roads of Lunigiana, the region in Tuscany, Italy, that is home to Montereggio.

The history of bookselling in the tiny hillside village of Montereggio in Tuscany goes back several centuries, well before it held the sixth International Book Town Festival in 2008. Indeed, the first printing press was operated in the town by Jacopo da Fivizzano in 1471 and the first bookshop was opened there in the late 1490s by Sebastiano da Pontremoli. Over the next 100 years, increasing numbers of local residents – sometimes entire families – began to operate as itinerant booksellers, toting huge wicker baskets of books around the local towns, visiting fairs and markets around central and northern Italy. The most popular titles initially were engravings and almanacs.

These ambulant sellers made their way gradually into the rest of the country and eventually even abroad into Europe and South America, as some turned themselves into publishers and booksellers with bricks and mortar premises. The work of families such as the Bertoni, Fogola, Ghelfi, Giovannacci, Maucci, Lazzarelli, Lorenzelli, Rinfreschi, and Tarantola is remembered in the many streets named after them throughout the town. In 1952, Montereggio hosted the inaugural Premio Bancarella, Italy's leading literary prize.

This gradual change was partly the result of the decline of the regional silk trade, forcing people to sell other goods. As well as books, the roaming salesmen and women also sold knives and other tools from their baskets. As the number and weight of the books increased, the sellers turned to using carts pulled by hand or by horses. Today, this history and the town's ongoing book activities are supervised by the volunteers of the Associazione Le Maestà di Montereggio, founded in 2013.

"It was very easy to get a licence to sell books as no rules existed. Merchants, junk dealers and illiterates could get one," explains the assocation's President Giacomo Maucci. "For example, in 1853, Montereggio resident Sante Maucci was a farmer, dentist, razor stones seller and bookseller."

By the time of Italian unification, intellectuals and richer members of society became particularly good customers, interested in banned books the ambulant booksellers were able to bring over the border from abroad. "The most requested books were those written by Mazzini, D'Azzeglio, Cattaneo, Rossetti, Pellico, Balbo but also erotic and romantic novels and the books written by Macchiavelli and Voltaire," says Giacomo.

Ironically, many of the booksellers were illiterate and probably only recognised books by their covers, which led to problems when books were republished by different publishers.

Today, this village of just fifty inhabitants hosts a huge book fair every August, and a prestigious illustrated book award to new unpublished titles, The Silent Book Contest. In addition to the several bookshops there are also many honesty shops, with piles of books arranged in niches and on tables scattered around Montereggio.

More information
- www.montereggio.it
- www.silentbookcontest.com
- Montereggio is in Lunigiana, in the province of Massa-Carrara. By car, it is around ninety minutes from Genoa, two hours from Florence, and two and a half hours from Milan.

Opposite above left: Ambulant booksellers Oreste Giovannacci and Maria Maucci pictured in France in 1920.

Opposite above right: Books line the city walls outside Montereggio.

Opposite below left: One of the many open air book stalls scattered around town.

Opposite below right: A street stall at the twelfth book festival.

Right: The town's statue, a salute to the itinerant booksellers.

MONTMORILLON
FRANCE

De la Trappe aux Livres...
has a healthy number of
bookcases and board games,
as well as 100 types of beer.

**The bridge over the
River Gartempe in
Montmorillon makes for
an ideal stall spot for local
tradespeople.**

With a population of around 7,000, Montmorillon is one of the larger book towns, or as it calls itself, La Cité de l'Ecrit et des Métiers du Livre (The City of Writing and Book Businesses). It certainly has a long association with printing and publishing – there were numerous paper mills in Montmorillon in the eighteenth century and the famous Rossignol educational posters which adorned classrooms around the country were produced here in the middle of the twentieth century.

It became one of France's *villes du livre* in 2000 thanks to financial support from the EU, local and regional authorities, and controversial local writer Regine Desforges known as the 'high priestess of erotic literature'.

"In the mid-1990s she was on the town council and suggested the book town theme be adopted for the restoration of the medieval quarter of the town," says Paul McShane, author of the report on book towns for the Churchill Trust. "Her proposal was supported enthusiastically by key political figures, not just on the town council but by levels of government extending all the way, it is said, to President Jacques Chirac. As a consequence, funding of more than six million euros was allocated to an extensive restoration of buildings, paving and signage for the new book town."

Its annual Salon de Livre book fair in June is enormous, attracting up to 100 authors for readings, exhibitions and workshops which are held not only in the central Place Regine Desforges but also around town, including in the local hospital chapel. Most of the colourful two dozen bookshops and related artists' studios are in the narrow streets of the medieval old town and include:

— Au Cri de la Chouette (Rue Champien) – good on regional and contemporary history
— Le Cheval Noir (Rue Bernard Harent) – unsurprisingly focuses on equine literature and related antiques
— Les Propylées (Rue Montebello) – science

Opposite left: The sign of a writer's shop.

Opposite above right: It's just a short walk from the bookshop to the local bookshop-cum-bar.

Opposite below right: Shoppers browse the book stalls in the shaded streets of Montmorillon in summer.

Below: The same street retains its bustle at night, with keen readers looking out for a bargain.

More information
- www.citedelecrit.fr
- www.salondulivredemontmorillon.com
- www.machines-a-ecrire.fr
- Montmorillon is in the Vienne department of the Poitou-Charentes region, an hour's drive from Poitiers, where there is also an airport, and just over half an hour by train.

and technology specialists, plus a stock of paintings and engravings
— Livres à vous! (Rue Montebello) – the place to get your Editions Rossignol
— Librairie de l'Octogone, (Place du Vieux Marché) – run by Frédérik Reitz, this concentrates on esoteric and human science titles. Frédérik is also editor-in-chief of the monthly *Magazine du Bibliophile*
— Les pieds dans les nuages (Rue Champien) – aromatherapy, feng shui, spirituality and nature titles
— Les Chants de Maldoror (Rue de la Poêlerie) – science fiction and fantasy, with magazines and comic books, including some in English
— Le Festin de Babette (Rue de la Poelerie, named after the film *Babette's Feast*) – food, wine and tobacco-related titles
— The Glass Key (Rue de la Poelerie) – run by James and Patsy Fraser, selling English literature, novels, poetry, detective novels, travel and biographies. The couple previously ran a secondhand bookshop in Hebden Bridge but moved due to rent rises

Details of courses and the bookshops run by artists around town can be found at the information centre La Préface (Rue Bernard Harent) where English-speaking staff are also available. Among the most popular are:
— ARTelier de la Gartempe - offers courses in calligraphy, painting and ceramics.
— L'atelier du Potier (The Potter's Workshop) – medieval illumination workshops for children and adults
— Au Coeur du Papier – document restoration
— Utopiarts – Chinese calligraphy
— Atelier Carl'arts – Medieval miniatures courses

As well as temporary exhibitions around town, there is also L'Aventure de la machine à écrire et à calculer, a museum featuring around 200 typewriters (and calculators), and even bar bookshops such as De la Trappe aux Livres which has a healthy number of bookcases and board games as well as 100 types of beer.

Indeed, it's not all about the book. Montmorillon is also famous for its macarons and even boasts a museum dedicated to the sweet treat.

MONTOLIEU

FRANCE

Today there are around a dozen bookshops... and a similar number of painters, sculptors, photographers and book craftsmen and women.

The view from the bridge in the picturesque mountain town of Montolieu.

In a high hilltop ravine setting that competes with Fjærland (see page 53) for most picturesque book town location, Montolieu was intended to be much more than simply a village of bookshops.

Its success is largely due the unstinting efforts of Michel Braibant. A bookbinder from nearby Carcassonne, he was determined that, as well as selling books, the town should celebrate their production, cultural importance and the importance of the arts in general. The town still describes itself as a 'Village du livre et des arts graphiques', and is proud that around twenty nationalities are represented in Montolieu. Among its residents is reclusive writer Patrick Süskind, author of the bestseller *Perfume: The Story of a Murderer*. Novelist Kate Mosse also set her short story 'Sainte-Thérèse' from *The Mistletoe Bride* collection in Montolieu.

Overall, more than fifty buildings were extensively renovated and turned into businesses and accommodation to welcome the new visitors – around 50,000 a year plus several thousand students – to this village of 800 residents. The old paper mill in nearby Brousse was restored and turned into a working business harking back to the time in the seventeenth and eighteenth centuries when Montolieu was the leading paper producing town in the area.

The regeneration was such that the village was also able to reopen its primary school and attract new businesess, including International Inkwell's Hotel for Writers. Today there are around a dozen bookshops, including Les librairies Le Dilettante (Impasse du Ferradou), which also has a branch in Paris, and The English Bookshop which is now on the first floor of the Librairie Abelard (Rue de la Paix). There is also a similar number of painters, sculptors, photographers and book craftsmen and women making handmade paper, restoring books, running marbling and bookbinding lessons, as well as creative writing courses such as the poetry 'working holidays' at The Montolieu Workshop.

Above left: Abélard on Rue de la Paix.

Below left: Playful painted window shutters appeal to younger readers.

Below: The charming Librairie du Centre on Rue Saint-André.

Officially opened as a book town in 1990, Braibant's hard work received active support from Richard Booth and Noel Anselot (the driving force behind the establishment of Redu book town) who both set up bookshops in Montolieu. Initially there was no strong local support for the plan – in fact there was an element of opposition among residents and councillors. Sadly, Braibant died in 1992, just as the project was starting to take off.

The Musée des Arts et Métiers du Livre, also known as the Musée Michel Braibant, is at the centre of the book town's activities. It examines the history of writing and exhibits old presses, and runs very popular courses for schoolchildren in printing, typography and papermaking. The L'Atelier du Livre in the former Manufacture Royale textile factory offers a similar range of activities, looking at all aspects of book production.

La Coopérative-Collection Cérès Franco

An indication of the success of Michel Braibant's cultural vision for Montolieu is the transformation of this former wine co-operative into a world class gallery, focusing on twentieth century artists. As well as a colourful permanent exhibition formed from collector Cérès Franco's personal collection, there are regular temporary exhibitions drawing visitors from around the country and abroad. Located on Route d'Alzonne, it is open from the end of April to November, from Tuesday to Sunday.

La Coopérative-Collection Cérès Franco – a former wine co-operative, now world class gallery.

More information

- www.montolieu-livre.fr
- www.lacooperative-collectionceresfranco.com
- Montolieu is in the Aude department in southern France. It is an hour by road from Toulouse which also has an airport and international train station. Carcassonne is south-east of Montolieu and half an hour away by car.

ÓBIDOS
PORTUGAL

One of the most stunning bookshops is the Grande Livraria de Santiago... Books in various languages crowd onto former altars and bookshelves have replaced pews.

The charming rooftops of Óbidos town.

Óbidos in Portugal is a beautiful and historic hilltop town; King Alfonso V married his cousin Isabella of Coimbra here in 1441. A fortified wall encloses a compact medieval town centre filled with cobbled streets and traditional houses.

The town was previously best known for its annual chocolate festival and as the home of the cherry-based liqueur, Ginjinha. That is, until José Pinho, owner of the popular Lisbon bookshop Ler Devagar (Read Slowly, Rua Rodrigues de Faria), had the idea to change Óbidos into a book town.

Óbidos stands out from most other book towns in that, rather than opening up new bookshops, many stores have simply added bookselling to their normal business. So the local art galleries sell art books, the Óbidos Biological Market (the former refectory of the town hall) has placed shelves of cookbooks behind its fresh fruit and vegetables, and the museums stock history, interior design and heritage titles according to their individual focus. Similarly Livraria da Adega

(Rua da Porta da Vila), once a wine cellar and now part of a larger coworking space, also has a good selection of books alongside its wine bar.

The Literary Man hotel (Rua D. João d`Ornelas), run by the town's former mayor Telmo Faria, has merged accommodation and literature particularly well. Around 50,000 books are for sale, spread around the thirty-bedroom location. There are plans to double that number, helped partly by donations from visitors. Some books are in Portuguese but most in English, with an emphasis on Penguin, Pelican and Pan Books.

There have also been a number of conversions. One of the most stunning bookshops is the Grande Livraria de Santiago, housed inside the town's thirteenth-century church next to Óbidos's impressive castle. Books in various languages crowd onto former altars, and bookshelves have replaced pews. O Bichinho do Conto (Estrada dos Casais Brancos) is the country's first bookshop devoted to children's

titles, housed in a former primary school. It is also experimenting with publishing its own books. The impressive post office building is now a bookshop, and elsewhere the Galeria Pelourinho (Rua Direita) has a good stock of poetry and works by Fernando Pessoa, while Residência Josefa de Óbidos (Rua Dom Vaso Mascarenhas) concentrates on photography titles.

Like Hay-on-Wye, Óbidos also hosts a major international literary festival, FOLIO, attracting highly regarded authors such as Salman Rushdie and VS Naipaul and featuring reading marathons, concerts, and screenings. Other projects include a scheme for turning abandoned houses into live-work spaces for writers, artists and other creative entrepreneurs.

Óbidos, which has around 3,000 residents, is a member of the International Organisation of Book Towns and was also named a City of Literature in 2015 by UNESCO (see page 171 for a full list).

Above: Óbidos Biological Market, where you can browse a cookbook and pick out the ingredients on the spot.

Left: O Bichinho do Conto, which specialises in books and events for children.

Right: The Literary Man hotel, home to thirty bedrooms and 50,000 books.

The oldest bookshop in the world

According to the Guinness Book of Records, the Livraria Bertrand in Lisbon is the oldest bookshop in the world still in operation. It was established in 1732 (though it moved location in 1755 after earthquake damage, before returning to Rua Garrett in the Chiado area) by Peter Faure, and gradually became an important hangout for intellectuals and writers such as Eca de Queiros. Pierre Bertrand joined Faure in 1742 and also married his daughter, taking over (and renaming the shop) with his brother Jean Jospeh when Faure died in 1753. After various changes of ownership over the centuries, an expansion programme started in the 1960s, and it now operates a chain of more than fifty bookshops around the country.

The blue-tiled exterior of the oldest bookstore in the world, Livraria Bertrand.

More information
- www.vilaliteraria.com
- www.obidosvilaliteraria.com
- www.foliofestival.com
- www.bertrand.pt
- Óbidos is forty-five minutes from Lisbon by car, and an hour by bus from the Campo Grande bus station.

PAJU
SOUTH KOREA

'Rainbow Publishing House was established with the dream of telling the stories of the ordinary people who helped create today's Korea.'

DaeWha Kang

The 100-year stair at Rainbow Publishing House glows at dusk in Paju.

Paju Book City stands alone among members of the International Organisation of Book Towns in that while it has bookshops, book cafés and publishers, it has nothing else but. Every single building and person here is dedicated to making, publishing, selling and promoting Korean books (the cafés do sell coffee too).

It is also located in perhaps the most unlikely location of any book town – the reclaimed marshy flood plain near the Korean Demilitarized Zone, just half a dozen miles south of the border with North Korea. Indeed, the siting of Paju Book City was a guiding principle by the founding publishers who wanted to emphasise the importance of the common good above self-interest. While at its heart was a commitment to print, the plan was to build somewhere as an antidote to the perceived overdevelopment of Seoul, a spot which put humanity and historic cultural values first and worked in harmony with the natural wetlands in which it operated. "It is not hyperbole to claim that this is one of the most extraordinary and most unsung cultural and architectural developments in the world," design critic Edwin Heathcote wrote in the Financial Times in 2009.

Since 1989 major international architects and designers have been engaged in turning Paju into a unique site. There is a traditional Korean 'hanok' house at the centre of the buildings, a symbol of the goal to ensure Paju is in harmony with its surroundings. It has been criticised as a slightly sterile industrial park, but others have applauded its quiet, tree-lined, largely traffic-free streets dotted with wooden benches and unusual features, such as the miniature railway which runs around the children's bookshop Alice's House.

There are book cafés everywhere, including the popular Hesse on the third floor of the Pinocchio Museum (Hoedong-gil). The vast Book House Foresta (Heyri) is a cultural arts complex on three floors where you can sip house-roasted coffee against a backdrop of floor-to-ceiling bookshelves.

The brainchild of publisher Yi Ki-Ung, but now owned by Korea's Ministry of Culture, Sports, and Tourism, today there are around 250 publishers based in Paju and 10,000 people working here (though very few live here and most commute in, some in special buses owned by publishers). It is divided into three zones – a Publishing District, a Printing District and a Support District. Books – mostly Korean but some in English and Japanese – are sold from the ground floor premises of various publishing companies as well in bookshops. As well as its annual Booksori book festival, which attracts up to half a million visitors over a week and a half of events, there are the Paju book awards for Asian writers, editors and designers for promoting the region's culture.

There is a remarkable dedication both to the history and the future of print in Paju. The Moveable Type Workshop is a working printers, producing collections of Korean poetry and furnished with endless shelves stuffed with lead type. It is also a reminder that Korea was using moveable-type printing methods 200 years before Gutenberg. Meanwhile, the Forest of Wisdom (Hoedong-gil) features eight-metre-high shelves and a collection of 50,000 donated books, many provided free by academics and other specialists. Volunteer book advisers help readers search the stacks, and there is also an on-site hotel, so visitors can read books twenty-four hours a day. Lectures and book clubs are run throughout the year, and in May Paju hosts a children's book festival.

The 100-year stair at Paju Book City

"Rainbow Publishing House was established with the dream of telling the stories of the ordinary people who helped create today's Korea," says its designer, DaeWha Kang.

"During the twentieth century, Korea was devastated by a period of colonial occupation, the Second World War, and the Korean War. From the extreme poverty of that time, the country has become one of the wealthiest and most advanced countries in the world. Although famous leaders were important for that transformation, there are also countless stories of ordinary people who lived extraordinary lives while rebuilding their country. Rainbow Publishing House takes its name from the idea that although each of those ordinary lives may be a small spark of light, when seen as a whole the many sparks create a colourful rainbow.

"The 100-year stair forms the main façade of the building. A bookshelf rises over four stories, with one shelf for each of the years of the twentieth century. The main stair wraps around the bookshelf, and a tall window gives views over all of Paju Book City. As Rainbow publishes small print run biographies of the people who lived through Korea's rebuilding, the books will be placed on the shelves corresponding to the year in which each person was born. Over time, the shelf will fill with the stories of Korea's rebirth, and all who use the building will be taking a journey through those histories and those lives as they take the stairs.

"The founders of Rainbow Publishing House live on the top floor, and one of our motivations for making the stair a beautiful and prominent feature was to encourage stair climbing rather than use of the elevator. Recent medical research has found a direct correlation between stair climbing and mortality rate, with those climbing five flights of stairs a day living 18 per cent longer than others. Giving beautiful views of the book city and a meaningful anchoring of books makes the staircase a more attractive option and encourages healthy living. An interactive tablet at the top of the stairs allows each of the four family members to tap in after taking the stairs, automatically recording the day and time they climbed. The display shows their progress and allows each a healthy competition with the others for who can do more. The tracking of this data is presented over time, telling the story of the family's health and activity over the years and decades. In this way, the story of a healthy and growing family is told in the same space as the story of a publishing house and of a country."

More information

www.pajubookcity.org (in both Korean and English)

Paju is 20 miles north of Seoul, about forty minutes by car.

Below: The Korean 'hanok' house in the centre of town, an architectural representation of the desire for harmony among people and place.

Bottom: Kyomunsa specialises in scientific publishing and uses this building as both its office and book warehouse.

Right: Two customers enjoy coffee surrounded by walls of towering books at Book House Foresta.

Below right: The spiral staircase staff entrance at Kyomunsa publishers, designed by Daniel Valle Architects.

REDU
BELGIUM

Rimbaud, Verlaine and Petrarch all enjoyed rambling around the surrounding Ardennes area.

The town church spire peeks above the trees of leafy Redu.

"There's an old lady who comes from La Louvière by train, then changes at Namur, goes down to Libramont and takes the bus to Redu," says Marie-Rose Bauvir who runs the Librairie Ardennaise bookshop (Rue de Saint-Hubert) in this Belgian book town. "She visits the bookshops and buys as many books as she can each visit and says as she leaves: "See you next year, if I can!""

Redu has certainly been one of the success stories of the book town movement since it became the first in continental Europe. The founding father was writer and oil industry executive Noël Anselot who was inspired by various visits to Hay-on-Wye in the late 1970s on fishing holidays. He opened his own bookshop in Redu in 1980, largely using books bought from Richard Booth in Hay (the two towns are now twinned). Anselot became a well-known international advocate of book towns, advising on the setting up of others around the world, including Montolieu in France (see page 95) and

St-Pierre-de-Clages in Switzerland (see page 115), as well as the shortlived one at Kampung-Baku in Malaysia in the 1990s. He was also one of the key consultants in the selection of Wigtown as Scotland's book town. In 1997, he received the Legion of Honor for his cultural commitment. Anselot was ably assisted in establishing Redu as a book town in 1984 by journalist Gérard Valet and the Mayor of Redu, Léon Magin.

The area certainly has plenty of literary connections – Rimbaud, Verlaine and Petrarch all enjoyed rambling around the surrounding Ardennes area – as do several of the bookshops. Fahrenheit 451 (Rue de Saint-Hubert) is unsurprisingly strong on science fiction, while De Eglantier (Rue de Transinne), owned by Miep Van Duin, has a whole floor of books in English in a kind of bookshop-within-a-bookshop called Crazy Castle. Its name was inspired by Skelton Castle in Yorkshire, owned by John Hall-Stevenson, a close friend of Laurence Sterne, which had an impressive library. The rest of the shop offers books in various languages, including Esperanto.

Like various other shops in Redu, De Eglantier is a renovated stable. A traditional farming village, the plan to become a *village du livre* was an attempt to fight its growing economic downturn, as with various other book towns. Local residents, many of them former farmers, were happy to offer their unused barns as shop premises. After a series of successful book fairs, the local council offered favourable rates to booksellers who renovated unused shop premises. At its peak there were twenty-five bookshops, attracting around 300,000 people a year. These numbers have fallen since then, but there are still a dozen booksellers, all with specialist genres: The Malle aux BD (Rue de Daverdisse) – graphic novels and *bandes dessinées* (comic books); Le Secret and La Barque Saoule (Rue de l'Esro) – children's books; L'archiviste (Rue de Saint-Hubert) – archaeology and heraldry; Le mât de cocagne (Rue de Hamaide) – crafts and music; Près d'elle (Rue de Transinne) – nature and health; De Griffel (Rue de Transinne) – gastronomy and folklore.

As well as focusing on the history of religion and Africa, The Librairie Ardennaise occasionally publishes *Le Journal de Redu* magazine, has a small art gallery and runs Le Musée des Imprimés next door. "Its aim is to trace the history of printing in the Province of Luxembourg from 1760 to the present day," explains Marie-Rose Bauvir. "Particularly popular for school groups is the

room which recreates a printing workshop with machines in working order. The children can get an idea of the evolution of print over the centuries up to the days of the computer."

There is certainly a hands-on feel to Redu. René Lefer, who once worked with Noël Anselot, produces handmade recycled paper and runs regular demonstrations. Meanwhile Roland Vanderheyden is the third generation of his family to run a bookbinding business, and also offers courses and internships. Redu has also been the headquarters for the Des Livres pour l'Afrique charity which collects French-language books and distributes them to African schools and libraries.

The book town is still very much alive. Anthe Vrijlandt and Johan Deflander came to Redu in 2015 and bought the La Reduiste bookshop (Rue de la Prairie), turning it into a literary vegetarian café and hotel (each of the three rooms has a large collection of books), which also hosts art events.

Below: A book-themed flowerbed welcomes visitors to Redu.

Opposite above left: Tourists take their pick from a couple of the bookstands dotted around town.

Opposite below left: This bookshop pays tribute to Ray Bradbury's famous work, and specialises largely in all things science fiction.

Opposite above right: René Lefer hard at work making paper.

Opposite below right: A woman browses the extensive collection of one of Redu's bountiful book stores.

More information

- www.redu-villagedulivre.be
- Redu is handily placed for various countries – it's easily reachable from south-east Germany, northern France (Charleroi is an hour's drive), as well as Brussels and Luxemburg. The nearest train station is Libramont. The Euro Space Center science museum is only three miles away.

RICHMOND
SOUTH AFRICA

'We are in a truly remote location... When people say it is such a long drive to get to Richmond, I reply that if you want to go to the moon it takes time!'

Peter Baker

A colourfully clad book printer and publisher in Richmond, located on the main road through town. Signage on the left points towards guest houses and useful stores in town.

Situated in the semi-desert wilderness of the Karoo, with very low rainfall and extremes of high and low temperatures, Richmond in the Northern Cape of South Africa is surrounded by mountains and plains, quite a contrast to the lush rural locations of most European book towns.

"We are in a truly remote location," agrees Peter Baker, co-founder of Booktown Richmond, "but still manage to get very good attendance to our events. When people say it is such a long drive to get to Richmond, seven hours from Cape Town and eight from Johannesburg, I reply that if you want to go to the moon it takes time!"

Richmond – the first book town in Africa – certainly has an out-of-the way feel to it. "The 'Karretjies Mense' cart people are an integral part of the town," says local resident Michael Drysdale, who works as an artist and writer. "They were originally the travelling sheep shearers who used to travel from farm

to farm. They are more settled now, but still come into the village to do shopping and to attend church."

The other guiding force behind Richmond's literary odyssey is longtime Afrikaans lecturer Darryl David, who has also set up other literary festivals in the region – the Schreiner Karoo Writers Festival in Cradock and the Midlands Meander Literary Festival in KwaZulu-Natal province. Darryl, who describes himself as "a child of the Karoo" chose Richmond partly because on his shortlist of potential locations in the region it was the only one with affordable property, and also because others simply showed no interest in the project.

Despite its location and size, Richmond's annual Bookbedonnerd literary festival in October has attracted some big names. Though it does receive some state funding, this has recently been slashed. It also has three well-stocked bookshops – Richmond Books and

Left: The headquarters of the Richmond Book Town association.

Below left: The 'Karretjies Mense' cart people, an integral part of the community in Richmond.

Below right: Classic Books, one of Richmond's three bookshops.

Opposite above: An aerial view of the nearby town of Philippolis.

Opposite below: The Van der Post Memorial Centre, where the writer, traveller and mentor to Prince Charles, Laurens van der Post was born.

Prints, Classic Books, and The Book Orphanage (all on Loop Street). Richmond Books and Prints specialises in Africana and especially early travellers, explorers, and missionaries. It is also architecturally interesting, made up of four Karoo-style houses and various converted stables and outbuildings. It also has impressive opening hours for such a remote location; Monday to Saturday from 9am-5pm and on Sundays by appointment.

Richmond is not vast, but in addition to the bookshops there are four restaurants open all year (and one which only opens during the annual book fairs), two coffee shops (again, one open only for book fair events) and three art galleries, including a ceramic pottery and sculpture studio. There is also a museum dedicated to saddle horses.

Philippolis

A mere two hours down the road from Richmond is Philippolis. Not only does it have a good restaurant-bookshop Oom Japie Se Huis, it is also home to the Laurens van der Post Memorial Centre (both on Voortrekker Street). The writer, traveller and mentor to Prince Charles was born here and his ashes are still kept there. The museum holds a collection of his works and exhibitions about his life, as well as the study in which he worked. There is also a studio available to artists, musicians and researchers which doubles up as a guesthouse.

More information

- www.richmondnc.co.za
- KZN Literary Tourism www.literarytourism.co.za is a good regional resource
- Richmond is on the main N1 roughly half way between Cape Town and Johannesburg (each a day's drive away) and between the major Karoo towns of Colesberg (an hour by car) and Beaufort West (two hours).

ST-PIERRE-DE-CLAGES
SWITZERLAND

St-Pierre-de-Clages is in the French-speaking area of Chamoson in the Swiss Alps, and as you'd expect, the views are quite spectacular.

A labyrinth of books for sale in the centre of St-Pierre-de-Clages.

Among the village of St-Pierre-de-Clages's book-based attractions is the opportunity to take part in *balades cyclolittéraires* (cycloliterature). Sita Pottacheruva is the creator of these tours, including several self-guided ones, which combine reasonably gentle cycling with literary landmarks (two combining wine and nature can be downloaded from the book town's website). Visitors can simply hop on a bike either in the main car park on the road to Riddes or from the Tourist Office, and ride free for up to four hours. St-Pierre-de-Clages is in the French-speaking area of Chamoson in the Swiss Alps, and as you'd expect, the views are quite spectacular.

In terms of bookshops, along Rue de l'Eglise you will find Le Fouineur (The Nosey Parker), which has a good general secondhand stock and La Plume Voyageuse (The Travelling Pen) run by Anne-Laure Berrut is dominated, as its name suggests, by travel, and ornithology

(books in French, English and German). It holds regular exhibitions of art and handicrafts. La Maison du Livre is also home to the specialist Le Coquuelicot (The Poppy) which describes itself as a 'librairie aromatique' and is particularly focused on esoteric and spiritual subjects as well as travel. It also sells essential oils and similar health products. Le Livre Ouvert (The Open Book) concentrates on similar subjects, including astrology, psychology and personal development.

As in other book towns, the main highlight of the year is the annual book fair, held in St-Pierre-de-Clages every last weekend in August. Around 100 publishers run stalls and there are demonstrations by calligraphers, illustrators and artists plus origami workshops for the children. The fair also holds a national spelling competition.

The Association Les Amis de St-Pierre helped to set up the book town following a visit

Left: A view towards the surrounding Apline hills.

Opposite above left: La Maison du Livre is also home to the specialist Le Coquelicot, which sells books on spiritual topics.

Opposite below left: There is always stiff competition for The Most Beautiful Swiss Books prize.

Opposite above right: Inside La Plume Voyageuse, which houses a wonderful collection of books on travel and ornithology.

Opposite below right: All manner of buildings and alcoves are requisitioned for the annual book fair.

to Redu and with the help of Richard Booth and Noël Anselot. It held its first book fair in 1993 and the tenth International Festival of Book Towns in 2016. Its free Literary Saturday events are popular public gatherings where around half a dozen invited authors discuss their work.

The Most Beautiful Swiss Books

Any book designed by a Swiss designer, or with a publisher or printer with headquarters in Switzerland, is qualified to enter the annual Most Beautiful Swiss Books competition. An international jury of experts chooses from a selection of several hundred entries to reward the best national book designs, based on the graphic design and typography as well as the quality of the binding and printing. No prize money is awarded, although a catalogue featuring the judge's picks is produced, and exhibitions of the winners are held around Switzerland and abroad. The competition was set up by the Swiss Association of Booksellers and Publishers but is now run by the Federal Office of Culture.

More information

- www.village-du-livre.ch
- www.swissdesignawards.ch
- St-Pierre-de-Clages is just under two hours from Geneva by train or car and an hour from Lausanne. The nearest airport is Geneva-Cointrin.

SEDBERGH
ENGLAND

Just out of town is former textile mill Farfield Mill, now an arts and crafts centre with more than a dozen resident artists, spinners and weavers.

Grazing sheep share field space with competitive cricketers outside the Cumbrian town of Sedbergh.

While many book towns were set up as an antidote to general economic malaise, Sedbergh did so in 2003 to counter a very specific issue – the decline in business due to the outbreak of foot and mouth disease. The goal was to widen the town's offering beyond its lovely countryside walks in the summer, though the concept did not appeal to everyone - antiquarian booksellers RFG Hollett & Son in Finkle Street decided to close its doors to the public rather than take part in the branding of Sedbergh as a book town.

Many of the booksellers in Sedbergh are multifaceted in their wares. Clutterbooks is the town's Community Charity Shop and sells secondhand books as well as games, puzzles and collectables. Profits are invested in a community fund which awards grants to local groups. Meanwhile, just out of town is former textile mill Farfield Mill (Garsdale Road), now an arts and crafts centre with more than a

dozen resident artists, spinners and weavers. It is also home to Avril's Books owned by Avril Whittle, which unsurprisingly specialises in craft and textile titles. The centre also organises the annual Sheepfest celebrations marking Sedbergh's history as a wool town – a recent theme was 'Book titles and characters'.

Elsewhere, Carole Nelson runs The Sleepy Elephant (Main Street), named after walker Alfred Wainwright's description of the Howgill Fells, which are very close to Sedbergh. It specialises in walking boots and essential hiking equipment, but also has a good range of local interest books, vintage children's titles, maps and guides.

Carole has been closely involved with the book town from the very start as one of its founding members, but still has some concerns about the future of book towns. "Craftsmanship will always be very popular. The actual physical object is not just something commercial, it's

a lovely thing," she says. "But we all need to think about how we can promote ourselves for the next century." One interesting move is a planned collaboration with Durham University to run a series of literary events linked to Anglo-Saxon literature on the theme 'From Beowulf to Brigflatts', a reference to the area's famous Quaker Meeting House.

Westwood Books (Long Lane) is by some distance the largest bookshop in Sedbergh, run from the former cinema by Evelyn and Mark Westwood who moved their bookselling business here from Hay-on-Wye in Easter 2005. It is the self-proclaimed 'largest bookshop in the Yorkshire Dales' and has tremendous views south and west over the Western Dales. Interestingly, none of its stock is available for sale on the internet. Here is their explanation: "While the internet can be very useful when searching for a particular title, it is no substitute for browsing a large and varied stock of real books. We believe that a large proportion of books bought in our shop were not known to the buyers before they found them here." In addition to an especially strong stock of books on the history of science, medicine and technology, Westwood Books also sells book-related gifts and cards over its two floors.

A key part to the book town's success is the Sedbergh Information and Book Centre on Main Street. Apart from its part-time manager,

Opposite: Outside Sedbergh Information & Book Centre.

**Left and above:
 A sign leads the way to Westwood Books, the largest bookshop in Sedbergh.**

it is staffed entirely by volunteers and run by Sedbergh Community Interest Company, which itself has a volunteer board of directors. "The building was originally 'Oakville', a family house, and for some time it was a National Park centre run by the Yorkshire Dales National Park Authority," explains manager Andi Chapple. "When the National Park decided to close the centre in the early 2000s, Sedbergh Book Town Ltd, realising that it was vitally important for a town like Sedbergh to have an information centre, took over responsibility for it. The CIC was formed when it became clear that the only way to keep the centre going was to rely on volunteers. Shelf space is rented to a number of book dealers, some of whom are volunteers at the centre. The centre's secondhand book sales are its bread and butter, along with sales of maps, new books and gifts. It is also involved in organising and publicising festivals and other town events."

Yorkshire Dales bookshops

In addition to those in Sedbergh are numerous secondhand bookshops dotted throughout the Dales – Sedbergh's information centre provides a useful Dales & Lakes Bookshop Trail guide for anyone looking to scout them out. One of the most controversial of these was Bloomindales in Hawes whose proprietor – once memorably described by a local councill as "the bookseller from hell" – at one point charged customers 50p to look around the shop. In response, Westwood Books temporarily offered to give anybody who bought a book in their shop 50p, the proceeds of which were largely donated by customers to Macmillan Cancer Support. Bloomindales closed its doors in the summer of 2017 and has reopened under new ownership as The Old Library Bookshop.

Left: Clutterbooks & Clobber is a community charity shop with a well-stocked range of literature.

Middle: Books share shelf space with walking sticks and boots – appropriate attire for a walk on the Dales – at The Sleepy Elephant.

Right: The interior of Sedbergh Information & Book Centre.

Opposite: Vintage everything; from nineteenth-century perambulators to lovingly worn secondhand books.

More information

- www.sedberghbooktown.co.uk
- www.sedbergh.org.uk/infocentre
- Most book shops are in Sedbergh town centre but Farfield Mill is a mile outside. Sedbergh is 12 miles from Kendal by road, and ten minutes by taxi from Oxenholme rail station, although the similarly distant Dent and Garsdale Head stations are both on the picturesque Settle to Carlisle line.

SELFOSS
ICELAND

Iceland is certainly an ideal country for a book town – its population of 330,000 are the keenest readers in the world.

Although Selfoss (population: 6,500) is the largest urban area in southern Iceland, it only really became a town in the twentieth century following the building of a suspension bridge that helped to unite its disparate parts. Today, as well as an agricultural centre and a good base for exploring the surrounding countryside, it is home to many commuters who work in the nearby capital, Reykjavik.

Iceland is certainly an ideal country for a book town. Its population of 330,000 are the keenest readers in the world, with around one in ten people publishing a book. Public benches include audiobook barcodes, and the Icelandic Literature Centre offers state support for Icelandic literature (including in translation). The country is also well-suited to the secondhand book trade as re-publication, even of bestselling books, is uncommon.

The book town project Bókabæirnir austanfjalls (Booktowns Iceland) is still in its infancy – it only launched officially in 2014 – and is led in particular by the Sunnlenska bókakaffið bookshop-café (Austurvegur) and the Konubókastofan in Eyrarbakki, a ten-minute drive away. Sunnlenska is the only bookshop in southern Iceland and is as popular for its cakes and coffee as for its stock of books in Icelandic, English and other languages. The Konubókastofan is a museum that preserves and celebrates female Icelandic authors, while also opening its doors as a workspace for aspiring writers.

The plan is not to focus all activity on Selfoss but, as with Tvedestrand (see page 145) and the Bokbyen ved Skagerrak (Skagerrak Book Town), to build up a network of likeminded partners, including libraries, in the surrounding area. This includes Hveragerði, only 10km away and known for its geothermal park, which became an artists' colony in the second half of the twentieth century. The annual children's

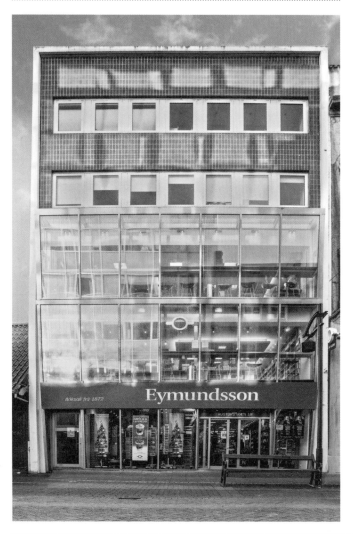

Left: Iceland's Eymundsson bookshop chain is particularly busy during Jólabókaflóð – the Christmas Book Flood.

book festival is a good example of how this works well, with events across the whole region.

Hveragerði and Selfoss (where singer Björk had a holiday home for many years, and where world chess champion Bobby Fischer is buried) are popular destinations for tourists, but the organisers of Bókabæirnir austanfjalls are hoping that the book town will not only create employment and promote Icelandic language and literature, but also enourage visitors to spend more money at local businesses.

Jólabókaflóð – The Christmas Book Flood

The most popular time to publish books in Iceland is between October and Christmas. There are huge numbers of book-related events in the lead up to Christmas Eve, on which the exchange of books as presents has become an annual tradition. To help people choose, households are sent a free catalogue – *Bokatidindi* – which features all new publications.

More information
- www.bokabaeir.is
- www.konubokastofa.is (Konubókastofan in Eyrarbakki)
- Selfoss is in the municipality of Árborg, 50km by road from Reykjavik, a UNESCO City of Literature (see page 171 for a full list) which holds its annual book fair in November.

Below: The Sunnlenska bookshop and café.

Bottom: Troll art located just outside of Selfoss.

Right: The warming interior of Sunnlenska bookshop and café.

Below right: Directions to the cities of Hella and Selfoss in southern Iceland.

SIDNEY
CANADA

Sidney on Vancouver Island, British Columbia, is Canada's only book town, established in 1996. Its pleasant seaside location makes it very popular with fishermen, and its population of 12,000 has a particularly high percentage of retirees.

Sidney's half-dozen secondhand bookshops (numbers have halved over the last few years but those that remain are still going strong) are clustered along Beacon Avenue. The street is home to the eponymous Beacon Books which offers a wide general stock as well as modern first editions and antiquarian titles, while a whole room is devoted to 'country living' titles. Galleon Books and Antiques is a non-fiction specialist, especially good on regional Canadian history and First Nation titles, as well as selling antiques and other collectibles.

As you would guess, The Military & History Bookshop, just off of Beacon Avenue on Fourth Street, is a military specialist, strong on the two world wars and Churchilliana. The Children's Bookshop caters for all youngsters from toddlers to young adults.

Tanner's is where the book town really started, when Clive and Christine Tanner opened their first bookshop here, now selling only new books. It also sells an incredibly wide range of magazines and newspapers from Canada, the USA and the UK, as well as many maps and nautical charts.

The Haunted Bookshop is named after Christopher Morley's 1919 novel of the same name (a bookshop-themed mystery tale rather than a supernatural whodunnit) and is Vancouver Island's oldest antiquarian bookshop with appropriately classic bookshelves. Established originally in Victoria in 1947 and run by Odean Long, it has an excellent children's classics section and also sells book ephemera, maps and prints.

In addition to these booksellers is the annual Sidney and Peninsula Literary Festival. Its organisers hold regular authors events throughout the year, and often stage talks with local publishers.

Above: The welcoming interior of Beacon Books, packed to the rafters with great tomes of literature.

Below left: War books for sale in The Military Bookshop.

Below: A sign in The Haunted Bookshop advises readers to find the owner where 'the tobacco smoke is thickest'.

This shop is haunted
by the ghosts
Of all great literature, in hosts:
    We sell no fakes or trashes.
Lovers of books are welcome here,
No clerks will babble in your ear,
    Please smoke – but don't drop ashes!

Browse as long as you like.
Prices of all books plainly marked.
If you want to ask questions, you'll
find the proprietor where the tobacco
smoke is thickest.
We pay cash for books.
We have what you want, though
you may not know you want it.
Malnutrition of the reading faculty is a
serious thing.

Let us prescribe for you.

The above from Christopher Morley's
"THE HAUNTED BOOKSHOP"

Munro's Books

Victoria is only a short drive down the coastline from Sidney, and home to several excellent bookshops including James Bay Coffee and Books (Menzies Street) which in addition to books sells vinyl, runs live music sessions, and serves vegan/gluten-free food. It is also the site of the headquarters of one of the leading names in online secondhand bookselling, AbeBooks.

It is also where you will find Munro's (Government Street), the bookshop set up in 1963 by writer Alice Munro and her husband Jim. Their first shop was on Yates Street and initially stocked mainly paperbacks, but since 1984 (and after a couple of relocations) it has been housed in an impressive neo-classical building originally built for the Royal Bank of Canada in 1909. Inside, high ceilings with sunken panels add to a traditional library feel. Munro's itself likens the ceiling to the porch of the great library in Ephesus, Turkey, built by the Romans around 114AD.

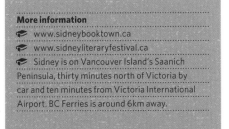

More information
- www.sidneybooktown.ca
- www.sidneyliteraryfestival.ca
- Sidney is on Vancouver Island's Saanich Peninsula, thirty minutes north of Victoria by car and ten minutes from Victoria International Airport. BC Ferries is around 6km away.

Outside the regal Munro's in Victoria, established by acclaimed short story writer Alice Munro.

STILLWATER
& TWIN CITIES
MINNESOTA, USA

Minneapolis has topped the country's annual Most Literate City survey, based partly on numbers of local bookshops.

Stillwater riverside in the early evening sunshine.

When does a book town cease to be a book town? There is a large grey area between a thriving bookselling community and the departure of the final business – but where there's a bookshop or two left standing, there's still hope.

Stillwater is an attractive river town in Minnesota and a popular historic destination for tourists, close to the Twin Cities Minneapolis and Saint Paul. It was also the first book town in the USA, officially recognised by Richard Booth in a visit in 1994 following an invitation from its two leading bookmen, Gary Goodman (of St. Croix Antiquarian Booksellers with its international reputation for maps and prints, as well as military and natural history titles), and Thomas Loome (of the eponymous Loome Theological Booksellers).

Around that time it had two dozen independent rare and used bookshops, its own publication, the *Stillwater Booktown Times*, a summer book festival and various other activities including seminars on book collecting and dealing. But hit by the rise in internet selling in particular, they have almost all closed down, including St. Croix Antiquarian Booksellers in the summer of 2017.

In the historic downtown area there is Black Letter Books, 'a real, honest-to-goodness brick and mortar bookstore,' Valley Bookseller (which only sells new books) and Loome (all on Main Street).

Thomas Loome opened Loome Theological Booksellers in the 100-year-old, abandoned former Old Swedish Covenant Church in Stillwater in 1983. It claims to be the largest secondhand dealer of theological books in the world, based around a stock built up from the dispersed libraries of Catholic seminaries, monasteries, convents, and other institutions which have closed down over recent decades. Among the collections it has handled are those of historian and former Dean of Christ Church, Oxford, Sir Henry Chadwick, and part of JRR Tolkien's working library.

Left: Garrison Keillor opened Common Good Books under Nina's Coffee Café on the corner of Selby and Western, Saint Paul.

Below left: The famous Amazon Bookstore Cooperative.

Below right: Inside Loome Theological Booksellers.

Opposite: A readers 'book construction' corner in Wild Rumpus Childrens Bookstore, Minneapolis.

More information

- www.booktown.com
- www.loomebooks.com
- www.openbookmn.org
- Stillwater is half an hour from Saint Paul by car and forty minutes from the Minneapolis-Saint Paul International Airport.

Loome is now run by Christopher Hagen, who started working at the bookshop in 2001 and then bought it in 2008 when Thomas Loome retired. It has since moved out to a farm location in Stillwater and then, because of rising rents, back into the main downtown area in July 2017. Despite the moves, the mission remains the same, with a stock concentrating on Catholic material but also anything scholarly that touches on Christianity. Christopher and his staff also advise other libraries around the world on building up their stock.

Twin Cities

Half an hour from Stillwater is the Twin Cities area, a national haven for bibliophiles. Minneapolis has topped the country's annual Most Literate City survey, based partly on numbers of bookshops, and Saint Paul regularly features in the top ten.

One of the most famous bookshops was the Amazon Bookstore Cooperative in Minneapolis. Established in 1970, it was the first lesbian/feminist bookshop in the country, later changing its name to the True Colors Bookstore. It was involved in a complicated trademark suit when Amazon.com was setting itself up, before eventually closing in 2012. The town still boasts a radical bookshop in the form of Boneshaker Books (23rd Avenue S), which runs the Women's Prison Book Project. The largest secondhand bookshop in Minneapolis is Magers & Quinn (Hennepin Avenue). Elsewhere is the Paperback Exchange (W 50th Street); James and Mary

Laurie Booksellers (3rd Avenue N), which also sells prints and vinyl records; the labyrinthine and marvellously-titled The Bookhouse in Dinkytown (SE 4th Street); and Eat My Words (13th Avenue NE), which supports local authors. Specialists in new titles include:

— Wild Rumpus (W 43rd Street) – children's
— Birchbark Books (W 43rd Street) – native American writers and literature
— Uncle Hugo's Science Fiction Bookstore and Uncle Edgar's Mystery Bookstore (Chicago Avenue)
— Once Upon A Crime (W 26th Street) – mystery
— Present Moment (Grand Ave S) – alternative subjects plus herbal medicines
— DreamHaven (E 38th Street) – science fiction and graphic novels

And lastly Open Book, a remarkable cultural centre with classes in book production, and the home of major publisher Milkweed Editions.

In Saint Paul, Midway Books (University Avenue W) is the leading antiquarian seller, but Sixth Chamber (Grand Avenue) has an excellent general stock. Among the sellers of new books is Common Good Books (Snelling Avenue S), owned by writer Garrison Keillor who created the famous fictional Minnesota town of Lake Wobegon. Red Balloon (Grand Avenue) and Addendum (S Cleveland Avenue) are especially strong on titles for young people.

SYSMÄ
FINLAND

Sysmä enjoys a beautiful lakeside setting.

Sysmä is positioned on the tranquil Lake Päijänne (Finland's deepest and second largest lake, containing water that is pure enough to drink). This, along with the outdoor delights of Päijänne National Park and the other 167 lakes in Sysmä, means that the permanent population of around 4,000 trebles in the summer.

The driving force behind establishing Sysmä as a book town in 1997 was Kerttu Tapiloa, a local art dealer who also ran an antique shop. The town is a founding member of the International Organisation of Book Towns, and held the biannual International Booktown Festival in 2002.

"The Sysmä Book Village Organisation organises an annual book fair in early July and also an event called The Night of Books, bringing readers, booksellers, and authors together from all over Finland," explains Raija Hänninen, Sysmä's head of tourism. "Some events take place at a local bookstore, which is perhaps the most beautiful bookstore in Finland.

"The local council has also renovated an old house, Villa Sarkia, named after the famous Finnish poet Kaarlo Sarkia who used to live in Sysmä during the 1940s. It is now used for residencies for young poets, authors and translators to stay in for a few months at a time at no cost."

Sysmä Bookvillage Ltd has also published more than forty books focusing on Sysmä. "Our biggest challenge is our quite unique language," says Raija. "Not very many people understand Finnish and few know much about Finnish literature. One of our most famous writers is Mika Waltari who wrote *Sinuhe, the Egyptian* in a tiny little cottage very close to us. Tours to that cottage are arranged once a year on Waltari's birthday in September."

Sastamala

One of the leading book events in Finland is The Days of Old Literature festival in Sastamala, three hours drive east of the the book town.

"The event lasts two days and always takes place on the weekend after Midsummer," explains Päivi Mäki-Kerttula, publicity manager for Sastamala. "For each festival there is also a theme – previously this has been Lapland, Helsinki, and literature's relation to movies. The event itself contains four different parts – secondhand bookshops, seminars, exhibitions focusing on the theme of the year, and exhibitors which are mainly stands of small publishers. There are around fifty secondhand bookshops and the same number of exhibitors. In 1986 there were about 1,000 visitors, and now it's up to around 15,000." The event is free for visitors.

More information
- www.sysmankirjakyla.fi
- www.sysmankirjakylayhdistys.fi
- www.vanhankirjallisuudenpaivat.com (Finnish only)
- Sysmä is in southern Finland, part of the Päijänne Tavastia region, two hours drive from Helsinki.

Above: Children at the monument to the famous Finnish book collector and author Eino Johannes Ellilä, who was born in Sysmä.

Left: Kirjakauppa bookshop in summer.

Above: One of a number of bookstores in town.

TORUP
DENMARK

**The singular architecture
of Torup book town.**

Torup is unusual even for a book town. There are two parts to the Danish community of around 300 residents – the old part (a village since the eleventh century), and a new zone that since the 1990s has been home to an eco-village called Økosamfundet Dyssekilde. It has its own health food shops, organic bakery, school, seven wind turbines, and dozens of sustainably-designed homes with solar panels. The original idea behind Økosamfundet Dyssekilde was to create a vegetarian, spiritual and humane village. After trying to work in many different directions during the start-up phase, the focus is now more on a shared foundation of beliefs and values than on a single concrete idea. The village is divided into six semi-autonomous groups who are responsible for the outdoor area between the homes and who manage their own budgets and social events.

University lecturer and resident Peter Plant, now the book town's chairman, heard a radio programme about Fjærland in Norway (see page 53) and believed it would be a good fit for Torup. After a visit to Tvedestrand (see page 145), Torup *bogby* (Danish for book town) was set up in 2006, and 2,000 people attended its first summer festival.

Five book wagons – little carts on wheels with canopies – were set up in 2007 to sit at roadsides for self-service use. This was joined by a book café in a greenhouse at the health food store Taraxacum, and a year later the village held its first writing workshop for aspiring writers. There are now a dozen book carts and places to buy books around town. In 2010 Torup became a member of The International Organisation of Book Towns, and in 2011 the restored former railway station dating back to 1916 became the book town's headquarters. There is now a bookstore on the ground floor as well as local food products and a bicycle rental station.

Secondhand books are donated for free. After a process of sorting, the best quality are put out for sale along the rural roads in and around the hamlet. Visitors will find mini bookshops in garages, a workman's hut, a disused stable, a farm entrance, in front of the church, and by the entrance to the supermarket. There are plenty of ingenious shelving ideas too, for example books stacked in bread boxes and milk crates. Some operate on a self-service honesty basis.

Residents can sign up as booksellers and choose from Torup Bogby's stock, usually selecting titles by specific theme or genre. Profits are then divided between the bookseller and the Torup Book Town Association. The Association runs a yearly Nordic Book Festival with talks and readings from established authors, along with music, and in 2009 a fringe film festival with contemporary Danish short films.

The organisers are keen to acknowledge that, while Hay-on-Wye is an inspirational example of sustainable rural development, Torup adds a social element to the concept of a book town. "The purpose of Torup Bogby is to create life," says Peter. "It strengthens the local community and the many cultural activities help build a richer spiritual life." Around twenty volunteers are closely involved with running the book town: sorting, distributing, and looking after the book carts; planning events; managing the website; and handling publicity and fundraising.

Ingstrup

There are now fourteen book trolleys in the streets of the much smaller Danish *bogby* of Ingstrup, situated on Route 55 in the rugged but scenic West Vendsyssel, on the opposite side of the country to Torup. One of its ongoing projects is to encourage residents and businesses to put up signs of sayings, quotes and proverbs on their buildings to literally 'spread the word' (and encourage people to visit local shops).

Left: Books for sale inside a renovated workman's hut.

Middle: An ad hoc bookshelf in the entrance to a barn.

Right and opposite: Roadside book carts dotted around town.

More information
- www.torupbogby.dk
- www.dyssekilde.dk
- www.ingstrupbogby.dk
- Torup is 60km north of Copenhagen, an hour and a half by train or an hour by road. The nearest major cities are nearby Hundested (7km) and Frederiksværk (5km).

TVEDESTRAND
NORWAY

Most of the town's secondhand bookshops are in the old quarter... where the rows of white wooden houses and steep, narrow cobbled streets are popular with tourists.

The captivating harbourside setting of Tvedestrand.

Tvedestrand proudly combines both book town status and a (brief) stint as a Guinness World Record holder. This picturesque harbourside town in Norway held the record for the longest chain of books toppled as dominos – its 6,500 in 2015 beat United Biscuits' previous high score of 5,370 (although this was overtaken a year later at the Frankfurt Book Fair with a grand total of 10,200).

The southern Norwegian book town has been officially known since 2003 as Bokbyen ved Skagerrak (as it is on the Skagerrak strait), and joined the International Organisation of Book Towns the following year. It is well supported financially, receiving state grants towards its work as well as sponsorship for everything from its website to its annual Bokbysommar children's book festival, from businesses and national writing organsiations such as the Norsk Forfattersentrum (Norwegian Writers' Centre). It also works closely with the Bokhottelet hotel,

which offers its space for the annual book festival – as does the Tvedestrand Fjordhotell – providing large numbers of books in all its rooms for visitors.

Tvedestrand is also the host of a popular annual crime festival run by bestselling Norwegian crime writer Hans Olav Lahlum, whose books have been translated into English as *The Human Flies*, *Satellite People*, *The Catalyst Killing* and *Chameleon People*.

Bokbyen Forlag is the publishing arm of the town's book association, publishing fiction and non-fiction, including local history and several focusing on maritime subjects, since 2006.

Most of the town's secondhand bookshops are in the old quarter, especially on the main street Hovedgata, down by the harbour where the rows of white wooden houses and steep, narrow cobbled streets are popular with tourists.

Bokbanken, the book town's HQ and publishing office, was previously home to a bank, and before that a distillery. It has a wide selection of books and plenty of activities for children in its 'Snipp, snapp snute' area.

Skagerrak Antikvariat (Hulgata) has a large stock of 70,000 books over three floors. It was initially based in Oslo before moving to Tvedestrand in 2003. Owner Arne Ivar Kjerland was a driving force in the Norwegian Book Town in Fjærland. The other major bookshop is Locus Antikvariat (Hovedgata), located in an old Swiss warehouse and run by Helge Baardseth, editor of the popular national travel magazine *Vagabond*. Unsurprisingly it's strong on travel and polar literature as well as architecture and design. Other bookshops include:

— Bjorn Dahl Bokmølle (Hovedgata) – history, local history, political history and biographies
— Ex Libris (Hovedgata) – ten rooms of general stock with a good English section
— Tvedestrand Bok & Papir (Hovedgata) – new books plus stationery, maps and gifts
— Familia Antikvariat (Arne Garborgsvei) – housed in the former dairy with a focus on hunting, fishing and nature books

The House of Literature
Norway is home to a remarkable ongoing project called Litteraturhuset (The House of Literature), run by the independent, not-for-profit Freedom of Expression Foundation, which describes itself as a 'democratic and pluralistic sanctuary'. Inspired by a similar movement in Germany, the first House opened in Oslo in 2007 in the city's former teacher training college, and is spread out over 3,500 square metres. Over its five storeys are a café, bookshop, performance spaces, an entire floor dedicated to children and young people (especially those from immigrant backgrounds) and another with fifty free spaces in which writers can work. There is even a rent-free apartment for visiting foreign writers on short stays.

The foundation's commendable aim is to promote literature in general and Norwegian and Nordic literature in particular, both fiction and non-fiction. It stimulates debate about books and the importance of freedom of speech via a busy programme of public meetings and seminars. There are now other literature houses in Bergen, Trondheim, Fredrikstad and Skien.

> **More information**
> ☞ www.bokbyen-skagerrak.no
> ☞ www.bokby.net (the town's online bookshop)
> ☞ www.litteraturhuset.no
> ☞ Tvedestrand is at the end of the Oksefjorden in Aust-Agder county, just over three hour's by car south from Oslo and an hour from Kjevik Airport in Kristiansand.

Above left: Oslo's House of Literature.

Above right: The sign for Bokbanken, the book town's headquarters.

Below left: A sign points towards a fellow book town, Wigtown in Scotland, just 900 kilometres away.

Below right: Former President of the International Organisation of Book Towns, Jan Kløvstad, reads to children in Tvedestrand.

URUEÑA
SPAIN

The only Spanish town with more bookshops than bars.

The city walls and winding streets of Ureña.

According to the latest Spanish census figures, Urueña has a population of just over 200, and has been dubbed the only town in Spain with more bookshops than bars by the country's national press. It also receives about 50,000 visitors a year.

It has one of the most dramatic of book town locations, set on top of a hill with huge twelfth- and thirteenth-century walls encircling the narrow streets, stone houses and marvellous 360-degree views across the surrounding countryside.

Officially declared Spain's first book town in 2007 (other candidates for the prestigious position included Maderuelo in Segovia, Montelalegre in Valladolid, and Candelario in Salamanca), the local authority restored various abandoned houses and offered them to booksellers and publishers who wanted to establish themselves in the town. The booksellers even receive a very small yearly stipend from the regional government.

The first bookshop was open by Jesus Martínez, who moved from Madrid to found Alcaraván (Corro de San Andrés) in 1992, specialising in ethnography and folklore. "It was the smallest village in Spain with a bookshop," he says proudly. As with all other book towns there have been closures and new arrivals. Libraria El 7 (specialising in the bullfighting books) has relocated to Madrid, a couple of hours travel south, while the newest bookshop is Primera Pagina (Corro Santo Domingo), run by international award-winning photojournalist Fidel Raso and journalist Tamara Crespo. It focuses on journalism, photography and travel, and runs events with famous writers such as Sharon Olds, winner of the 2013 Pulitzer Prize for Poetry.

Other bookshops include El Grifilm (Corro de Santo Domingo), specialising in cinema; La Bodega Literaria (Corro de Santo Domingo) – contemporary hispano-american literature, Generation of '27 authors, and medical books from the eighteenth century; and Páramo (Calle Lagares). Enoteca at Santa Domingo not only

Above: Outside the Alcaraván bookshop.

sells books about wine but also wine itself, and its exterior walls feature various famous quotes about the delights of the grape.

Special events including courses run by the village's specialists (calligraphy organised by Alcuino Caligrafía & Arte, and bookbinding run by the Taller de Encuardernacion), readings and concerts held on World Book Day, and the village's anniversary in March.

Urueña is certainly a remarkable small town. As well as the bookshops there are numerous museums and cultural centres. The Museo del Cuento (Museum of the Story, Calle Costanilla) has a permanent collection of art and sculpture by Rosana Largo, inspired by traditional stories such as Sleeping Beauty and Cinderella. It also holds an impressive display of pop-up books dating back to the nineteenth century and has its own bookshop.

The Centro e-LEA Miguel Delibes (Calle de la Costanilla) contains various workshop spaces, an extensive library, and a museum on the history of the book. As well as temporary exhibitions, there is a permanent one dedicated to experimental twentieth-century Spanish poet Francisco Pino. It also awards a biennial literary prize.

In addition there is the Joaquín Díaz Foundation (Calle Real) created by the musician and ethnographer himself, which holds around 26,000 books, a similar number of photographs and a huge collection of vinyl records, gramophones, and sheet music.

Inside Librería Páramo.

More information
- www.urueña.es/librerias-talleres-villa-del-libro
- Urueña is in the Valladolid province of Castile and León. Valladolid is 50km to the east, about fifty minutes by car with a direct bus connection and the nearest train station to the book town. The nearest airport is Villanubla, close to Valladolid.

WILLKOMMEN
FÀILTE
BIENVENU

Welcome to
SCOTLAND'S
NATIONAL
BOOK TO

WIGTOWN

SCOTLAND

'Becoming Scotland's book town has put us back on the map and given people a reason to come here.'

Andrew Wilson

The bowling green and Country Building in Wigtown, Scotland's only book town.

Wigtown offers the keen reader perhaps the most enticing of prospects, the chance of temporarily running a bookshop. The Open Book, set up by The Wigtown Festival Company on the high street in the middle of town, can be booked for up to a fortnight. Visitors stay in the flat above the shop at night and manage the business during the day. It's remarkably cheap (via Airbnb) but it is usually booked out months in advance. To get a flavour of the experience, the temporary booksellers are encouraged to contribute a diary of their stay to the shop's tumblr at theopenbookwigtown.tumblr.com.

The turnaround in Wigtown's fortunes has been remarkable. By the mid-1990s the decline in the local whisky distillery and creamery industries resulted in very high unemployment, numerous empty properties faced demolition, and grim prospects for the future. The turning point came when Wigtown beat five other locations (Gatehouse of Fleet, Moffat,

Dalmellington – which was Richard Booth's preferred choice - Dunblane and Strathaven) to become Scotland's official book town in 1998. Two decades later it is a thriving town again, popular among walkers for its beautiful rural location, full of secondhand bookshops, and home to one of the UK's major literary festivals. And the distillery has reopened.

The first festival took place in 1999, and the ten-day event in September and October now attracts more than 25,000 people. It caters for ages across the board with a special children's festival – Big DoG, named after Nana in Peter Pan - and another for teenagers and young adults. Over 200 authors take part in nearly 300 events each year, and there is an annual Spring Weekend in May as well as a poetry competition. Wigtown Book Festival is run by a small professional staff headed by Adrian Turpin who was awarded an OBE in 2017 for services to literature and the economy of Wigtownshire, but it would not happen on this scale without the hard work of around 100 dedicated volunteers.

"Becoming Scotland's book town has put us back on the map and given people a reason to come here," says Andrew Wilson who runs Beltie Books on Bank Street with its emphasis on all things Scottish, especially Covenanters and local football team Queen of the South. "The book town was important to us on deciding where to come and live. I wanted to move back to my home area and Wigtown's charm and the likelihood of there being more cultural activity convinced us to come here in particular. You will never become rich selling books, but as a second income for a family or as a step to retiring, having a bookshop is perfect. Wigtown as a book town definitely attracts a much more mixed and lively group of people than other similar small rural communities. It is an uphill struggle at times to come up with things to promote the place or bring the community together, but the whole concept of being a book town opens up lots of possibilities."

Like various other bookshops in Wigtown, Beltie also operates as a café and even offers accommodation. Glaisnock Café and Bookshop (Main Street) is as proud of its locally-sourced offerings and guest rooms as it is of its 'book cave' of general stock, and ReadingLasses (also Main Street) offers vegan and vegetarian food as well as 25,000 books in its shop and converted telephone exchange round the back.

"ReadingLasses is the only bookshop left in the UK specialising in Women's studies and books 'by and about' women," says Jacqui Robertson who bought the shop in 2015 after a career as a teacher and lecturer for more than 30 years teaching in far flung locations like the Falkland Islands and remote Scottish Islands. "ReadingLasses trades mainly in secondhand books and we boast a very large collection of Virago Press and Women's Press titles. We also have probably the largest collection of lesbian fiction in stock in any bookshop. I like to think of ReadingLasses primarily as quite a quirky women's bookshop. I am rather self-indulgent and only stock books about subjects I'm interested in so we have science, natural history, social science, travel and exploration, and history. My reasoning is that if I am knowledgeable about the subjects and books I can talk about them with customers. At the moment we are in the middle of renovating a huge barn at the back of the premises, and this will become an academic library containing reference books and journals. Writers will be welcome to use this as a retreat, we will be able to host events and run tutorials and study groups. There is further renovation work planned to provide a further venue space during the Book Festival. This is all challenging but, hey, what's life without a challenge!"

Wigtown is home to Scotland's largest secondhand bookshop, The Bookshop, run by Shaun Bythell, whose memoir *The Diary of a*

Bookseller details the delights and the challenges of running a secondhand bookshop. Also on Main Street is Byre Books which specialises in mythology and folklore – it also happens to have one of the most marvellously bucolic entrances to a bookshop in the world. And then there's The Old Bank Bookshop run by Ian and Joyce Cochrane. "I grew up just six miles up the road, went to school fifteen minutes down the road, then left for university." says Joyce, a chartered librarian. "It was the Book Town that brought me home." They sell a huge amount of sheet music, too, from their premises in the old Customs House and Bank, which dates back to the eighteenth century.

Among the various book publishers in town is the small, independent Curly Tale Books (also Main Street). It was set up by writer Jayne Baldwin and author and illustrator Shalla Gray in the former children's bookshop The Box of Frogs – they continue to sell books for younger readers as well as publish new titles.

More information
- www.wigtown-booktown.co.uk
- www.wigtownbookfestival.com
- www.theopenbookwigtown.tumblr.com
- Wigtown is in Dumfries and Galloway, two hours by car from Glasgow or Carlisle and just over an hour from Dumfries.

Opposite: The enchanting pathway entrance to Byre Books.

Above: There's something for everyone at the Wigtown book festival.

Below: The largest book town in Scotland.

WÜNSDORF
GERMANY

Around 6,000 people live in Wünsdorf today, but for most of the previous fifty years it was home to 75,000 Russians and a whole network of shops and schools.

Boats moored on the shores of Lake Steinhude in Wünsdorf.

No other book town has undergone such a complete rebranding as Wünsdorf. Once the former headquarters of the Wehrmacht (the German Armed Forces) this pleasant forested area is where the Nazis ran their campaigns, from inside the Zeppelin underground communications bunker. The German competitors in the 1936 Berlin Olympics also lived and trained here.

The buildings have protective walls more than a metre thick, as the Russian forces discovered when they captured it in 1945 and turned it into their German headquarters. Around 6,000 people live in Wünsdorf today, but for most of the previous fifty years it was home to 75,000 Russians and a whole network of shops and schools. Wünsdorf became known as 'Klein Moskau' ('Little Moscow'), except to the East Germans who were not allowed to enter without written permission, and so named it the 'Verbotene Stadt' (the 'Forbidden City').

In 1994, the Soviet troops (and their families) left Wünsdorf very suddenly and the town slowly disintegrated. The German authorities faced a huge clear-up job, with munitions scattered over more than 250 hectares, but German citizens have been returning to Wünsdorf, partly attracted by the low property prices. The town was rebranded as a 'book and bunker' town in 1997, and became a member of the International Organisation of Book Towns. It is now popular with bibliophile tourists as well as those intrigued by the old bunker system.

There are now three large antiquarian bookshops with a stock of around 300,000 titles combined. Gutenberghaus (Guthenbergstraße) houses the book town's main office, the Bunkershop (Zehrensdorfer Straße) specialises in military history and other military items, and Haus Oskar (also on Zehrensdorfer Straße) is the starting point for tours of the area, including the impressive bunker complexes (wear a jacket as they are always a bit chilly) and other military installations.

Above: The Bücher con sum bookshop in Muhlbeck.

Below left: Reinforced doors at the Bücherstall book stall.

Below: The famous statue of Lenin in Wünsdorf.

Germany's book towns

Germany's first book town was Mühlbeck-Friedersdorf in Saxony-Anhalt (45km from Leipzig), which hosted the second International Book Town Festival in 2000, during which the International Organisation of Book Towns was officially set up. There are now two general bookshops in the former school and another in the old rectory, while the Buch- und Luftfahrtantiquariat Girev (Dorfplatz) specialises in aviation, aerospace and missile technology titles.

Another *buchdorf* is Müllenbach in Rhineland-Palatinate, just over an hour's drive east of Cologne, two hour's north of Frankfurt. Here, Das Bücherkabinett is particularly good for children's books, H.A.M. for art history and travel, and Melzers Antiquarium for adventure titles. There are various book festivals throughout the year including a Robinson Crusoe Day in February.

Visitors to Wünsdorf will also enjoy a trip to nearby Berlin, especially the Christopher Isherwood Walking Tour which visits sites associated with him and his work as well as his former apartment. Bookshops to look out for include: Saint Georges English Bookshop (Wörther Straße); Hammlett Krimibuchhandlung (Friesenstraße) dedicated to new and secondhand crime and mystery titles, mostly in German and English; Dante Connection (Oranienstraße) fiction and non-fiction from and about Italy in Italian and German translation; Otherland (Bergmannstraße) – science fiction, horror and fantasy books in German and English; and Mundo Azul (Choriner Straße), a children's bookshop with books in German, English, French, Spanish, Italian, Russian and Portuguese plus workshops for younger and bilingual readers.

More information

- www.buecherstadt.com
- Mühlbeck www.buchdorf-info.de
- Müllenbach www.buecherdorf-muellenbach.de
- www.isherwoods-neighbourhood.com

Wünsdorf is just under an hour by car from Berlin (just over an hour by train) and half an hour from the BER Berlin-Schönefeld airport.

Below left: The Bunkershop and its appropriate decorations.

Below: A trilingual welcome to Wünsdorf.

BEYOND THE
BOOK TOWN

When is a book town not quite a book town? Whether a single
street in a bustling city or a pop-up spot during a literary festival,
the following locations have all the feel of a literary paradise,
just not the official title...

BHILAR

INDIA

Unlike other book towns, no books are actually for sale in Bhilar – it is more of a multi-location library.

A view of Krishna River Valley and Dhom Dam from Krishnabai Temple, Mahabaleshwa, just half an hour's drive from Bhilar.

Bhilar, in the Satara district of Maharashtra, became India's first book village or *Pustakanche Gaon* when it opened in May 2017. It was previously best known as an area which produces vast quantities of strawberries – 90 per cent of its 10,000 population work in the strawberry industry, which grows more than 85 per cent of the country's strawberries. Now, it offers around twenty-five locations along its 2km long main street where locals and visitors can borrow books for as long as they want after paying a token membership fee.

Unlike other book towns, no books are actually for sale in Bhilar – it is more of a multi-location library. Spread across three and a half acres, books are available in temples, schools, homes, and hotels. One contains around 15,000 books (plus magazines and newspapers) and counting.

Funding has come from the regional Maharashtra government rather than a groundroots booksellers' initiative. The state provides all chairs, beanbags, tables and bookshelves, as well as paying people rent to use their premises as spaces for reading. Improvements have also been made to the local road infrastructure.

The main aim of the book village, where around 600 families live, is to promote the region's Marathi language – one of India's twenty-two officially recognised languages (more than seventy million people speak it) – and also encourage tourism. It is certainly in a stunning location, close to the well-known hill stations of Panchgani, a popular summer resort during the British Raj especially for retirees, and Mahabaleshwar. The local authorities plan to run regular school trips to Bhilar for students across the state. Villagers hope that the increased numbers visiting the area as a result of the new designation will help boost the local economy, especially among Bhilar's two dozen hotels.

Unsurprisingly, most of the books – including around 2,000 for children – are in Marathi, but

the organisers are aiming to add another 25,000 in English, Gujarati and Hindi. The goal is to have around two thirds of books in Marathi, including some multilingual titles. Much of the stock is currently out of print.

As well as the books, walls around the villages have been painted by a group of seventy-five artists from nearby Mumbai and Pune, all members of a WhatsApp-based artist network called Swatva. The artwork will indicate which genres of books are contained inside the property, including history, literature, poetry, and religion. So, for example, books about Indian warrior king Shivaji Maharaj are advertised with paintings of forts. Each location tends to specialise in certain categories – visitors staying at Anmol's Inn will find books written by leading statesmen and famous celebrities.

There are also plans to run literary events, including workshops, author readings and a summer literature festival, as well as to establish a similar project in the Maharashtra coastal village of Malgund in Konkan, birthplace of the famous Marathi poet Keshavasuta.

More information

Bhilar is around 250km and a four and a half hour drive from Mumbai, two and a half from Pune. Panchgani is around 7km away. The nearest airport and railway station is at Pune.

Left: A local woman reads a magazine in front of one of the many colourful murals that adorn the village walls.

Opposite above left: An elderly man reads a book in the Marathi regional language.

Opposite above right: Reading corners are easy to come by in India's first 'village of books'.

Opposite below left: An elderly woman sits among the book displays of a local house in Bhilar.

Opposite below right: Indian women in traditional dress sample some of the 15,000 books made available for locals and tourists alike in Bhilar.

BUENOS AIRES
ARGENTINA

This city is so proud of its bookish heritage that it even offers a special pension scheme for writers.

Inside the incredible Ateneo – a book store housed in a former theatre in Buenos Aires, Argentina.

There are now twenty official UNESCO Cities of Literature dotted around the globe, but if only one could be awarded the honorary title of 'Book Town', Buenos Aires would be a strong contender. It has more bookshops per person than any other city in the world – around twenty-five for every 100,000 residents (Hong Kong is just behind).

Home to many famous writers including Jorge Luis Borges and Julio Cortázar, alongside its huge number of bookshops it also has countless publishers, literary cafés and bars, as well as an enormous annual international book fair which attracts more than a million visitors for its twenty-day duration every April to May. The city is so proud of its bookish heritage that it even offers a special pension scheme for writers. Several companies offer guided, literature-based walking tours in Buenos Aires.

Café Tortoni (Avenue de Mayo) is perhaps the most famous in Buenos Aires. Others include the Florida Garden Café (Florida) and La Biela (Avenue President Manuel Quintana), one of Borges' favourite cafés – writer Adolfo Bioy Casares was such a regular that he had his own table. Confitería London City (Avenida de Mayo) was one of Cortázar's favourite haunts, and it displays plenty of the novelist's memorabilia.

Avenida Corrientes is the bookshop hotspot, with many pavement sellers too. There is also a large book market on Sundays in Plaza Dorrego in the San Telmo district, and another in Plaza Italia throughout the week. Of the bookshops, the most internationally famous is El Ateneo Grand Splendid (Avenue Santa Fe). Originally a theatre built in the early twentieth century, its frescoed ceilings and intact theatre boxes now provide a spectacular backdrop for bookshelves (the stage is now a café). Walrus (Estados Unidos) is one of the best for secondhand English titles, and it also runs creative writing courses and poetry readings. Similarly atmospheric are Libros del Pasaje (Thames) and El Rufián Melancólico (Bolivar).

La Libería de Avila (Adolfo Alsina) is the oldest bookshop in Buenos Aires (and some claim the world), dating back to the end of the eighteenth century. More like a cultural centre than simply a bookshop is Dain Usina Cultural (Thames) it incorporates exhibition spaces, holds regular lecture series, and houses a popular bar.

There is also a growing tradition of *librerías a puertas cerradas* (closed door bookshops) which do not have traditional shop fronts. Best-known is Micasa, run from Nurit Kasztelan's home in the Villa Crespo area, and her own books (not for sale) are cheek-by-jowl with those which can be bought. She has a particularly good stock of titles from small independent publishers. Los Libros del Vendaval (Gral. Enrique Martínez) is run along similar lines and specialises in children's books.

The book art of Buenos Aires

To put it mildly, activist artist Raul Lemesoff's Arma De Instruccion Masiva (or Weapons of Mass Instruction) is not your average mobile library. Using an old 1979 Ford Falcon repurposed to look like a tank, Raul drives around Argentina – and in particular Buenos Aires – peacefully offering his stock of 900 books to passers-by. The Falcon was popular with the armed forces of the country's former military dictatorship – instead of representing oppression, it now delivers books of all sorts, restocked entirely through private donations.

Buenos Aires has also been home to one of the most unusual pieces of book art. In 2011, conceptual artist Marta Minujin built a 25-metre-high Tower of Babel out of 30,000 books donated by libraries, foreign embassies and members of the public to celebrate the city's naming as World Book Capital of the year. A special ramp allowed people to 'climb' the tower. In 1983, she built a similarly vast model of the Parthenon in a Buenos Aires park. It was made from books that had been banned during the dictatorship.

UNESCO Cities of Literature

All the cities granted special City of Literature status by UNESCO must show evidence of ongoing publishing, educational programmes, and literary events, and that books generally play a key part in the city's life. Edinburgh was the first and one of the busiest, but new cities are added at regular intervals.

Edinburgh, Scotland (2004)
Melbourne, Australia (2008)
Iowa City, United States (2008)
Dublin, Ireland (2008)
Reykjavik, Iceland (2011)
Norwich, England (2012)
Krakow, Poland (2013)
Heidelberg, Germany (2014)
Dunedin, New Zealand (2014)
Granada, Spain (2014)
Prague, Czech Republic (2014)
Baghdad, Iraq (2015)
Barcelona, Spain (2015)
Ljubljana, Slovenia (2015)
Lviv, Ukraine (2015)
Montevideo, Uruguay (2015)
Nottingham, England (2015)
Óbidos, Portugal (2015)
Tartu, Estonia (2015)
Ulyanovsk, Russia (2015)

More information

📖 www.librosdelpasaje.com.ar

📖 www.dainusinacultural.com

📖 The main international airport is 20 miles from the city centre with good rail, coach and underground connections. As well as the ubiquitous black and yellow taxis, there is also a free public bicycle scheme called Eco-bici which makes good use of the flat city's many bike lanes.

Above left:
The chandeliers at the Eterna Cadencia bookshop.

Above right:
An overflowing book stall at Plaza Italia.

COLLEGE STREET
KOLKATA, INDIA

The street's busy, often chaotic, character makes for a very colourful browsing experience.

Towards the end of the eighteenth century Kolkata (then known as Calcutta) became a major printing centre, largely thanks to the East India Company which built up the industry for commercial reasons. It has retained that pedigree, and the International Kolkata Book fair, estabished in 1976, is now the world's biggest book fair for the general public.

Though not an actual town, College Street in the northern, older part of the city has turned itself into a haven of bookselling in India. Known locally as 'Boi Para' or the 'Colony of Books', it is regarded as the largest secondhand book market in the world. Around 1.5km long, stretching from Mahatma Gandhi Road to Ganesh Chandra Avenue, it is home to a long stretch of streetside book stalls, traditional bookshops, publishers, and educational institutions.

The street is liberally sprinkled on both sides with numerous small open-air book stalls made from bamboo, sheets of tin, and canvas. Some of the booksellers claim a family tradition of bookselling here going back over 100 years. The stock is extremely eclectic – especially good for textbooks, it also stocks fiction and non-fiction, pamphlets and other printed ephemera, largely in Indian languages (particularly Bengali) and English. Combined with the street's busy, often chaotic character, it makes for a very colourful browsing experience. Be prepared to haggle good-naturedly over prices.

Among the 'bricks and mortar' bookshops are the National Bookstore (just opposite the Presidencey University, which is unsurprisingly well stocked with academic and textbooks), Dasgupa & Co (College Street's first bookstore, set up in 1886) and Bani Library (a family-run business for five generations).

One of the most famous landmarks along College Street is the Indian Coffee House, opposite the Presidency University, part of a

Below: The entrance to the famous Indian Coffee House, a meeting place for intellectuals, artists and politicians.

Right: Relaxed bookselling on College Street.

Below middle: Colourful bunting decorates the street, where a string of booksellers work side by side.

Below right: A roadside salesmen peddles books and magazines.

chain owned and run as co-operatives by its employees. Though not noted for the quality of its coffee, it does have an impressively long history as a meeting place for intellectuals, artists, and politicians, popular with figures such as Rabindranath Tagore, Amartya Sen and Subhas Chandra Bose as well as local students. Above the Coffee House is Boi-Chitra which puts on regular photographic exhibitions and specialises in rare books, CDs and magazines.

There have been longstanding plans to demolish part of College Street and replace it with an enormous book mall, but for now these have thankfully stalled.

More information

☞ www.kolkatabookfair.net

☞ College Street is accessible by car or tram. Netaji Subhash Chandra Bose International Airport is about 15km from the city and the city has good rail connections to most of the country's main stations.

Left: Medical books are the specialty at number 108 College Street.

Below: Bookselling, Kolkata-style.

JIMBOCHO
TOKYO, JAPAN

The area gradually developed its current specialism following a major fire in the area in 1913 and the earthquake of 1923.

Books half-inside, half-outside at The Yaguchi bookshop in Jimobocho.

Jimbocho is a book town within a city. Located mainly around the intersection of Yasukuni-Dori and Hakusan-Dori in the Kanda district of Tokyo, it is home to nearly 200 bookshops, publishers and related clubs and societies, such as the Literature Preservation Society and Tokyo Book Binding Club. It is arguably the largest secondhand book market in the world.

The area gradually developed its current specialism following a major fire in 1913 and the earthquake in 1923, surviving largely unscathed during Second World War bombings. Today, most of the bookshops are based on the south side to reduce sun damage to the books, although many have such a large stock that they have overflow tables on the pavement outside. 'Shoten' ('write shop') is the common term for bookshop – the two characters visitors should look out for are 書店.

As you would expect, every subject is covered in terms of stock, mostly in Japanese but also in English and to a lesser degree other European languages. So afficianados of Go or Shogi should head for the Akashiya bookstore, while those interested in science fiction and martial arts are well catered for at @Wonder. Elsewhere there is Isseido (woodblock-printed books), Vintage and Yaguchi (film and theatre), Okubo (natural sciences), Kagurobun, Yamada and Hara Shobo (Japanese art, especially 'ukiyoe'). Toyodo is well known for its collection of Buddhist titles. As well as manga (leading publisher Shueisha is located in Jimbocho) large numbers of bookshops stock Japanese *gravure idol* (glamour modelling magazines).

For English language titles, Ogawa Tosho is the best, along with Kitazawa, which was once the country's leading specialist in foreign language titles. Infinity Books is an English-language specialist run by longtime resident Nick Ward, which also hosts music and book events, enlivened by the bar in the centre of the

bookshop. Tamura Shoten holds a good stock of original French, German and Chinese literature. Books Sanseido is one of a major chain of bookshops in Japan with a very wide general stock and English titles on its second floor.

There has also been an annual Kanda Used Book Festival since 1960, with a particularly large outdoor book market. Pavements are lined with pop-up bookshops that sit opposite the permanent booksellers.

Bookish Tokyo

Haruki Murakami mentions Jimbocho in several of his books but there are also fascinating bookish delights outside the area. Among them is Book And Bed (Nishi Ikebukuro) which describes itself as an 'accommodation bookshop' – a hostel catering for around fifty people in bunk beds placed behind bookshelves (a cheaper option allows you to stay in more straightforward surroundings, but where's the fun in that?). It's not a luxurious sleeping experience, but the shelves do hold around 3,000 books in English and Japanese, which clients can peruse at will.

Elsewhere, Megu Tama (Shibuya) is a restaurant and café with an interior décor of 5,000 photographic books donated by photography historian and critic Iizawa Kotaro. Diners can take any book with them to the table and read while they eat (although none are for sale).

Left: Book and Bed, a hotel where you can sleep inside the bookcases.

Below left: Boxes of books line the streets of Jimbocho.

Below: The alleyway next to @Wonder.

Bottom: Labels identify the stacked volumes of a secondhand bookshop.

More information
- http://jimbou.info (Japanese only)
- http://bookandbedtokyo.com
- http://megutama.com
- The area has its own train/subway station called Jimbocho on the Tokuo Metro Hanzomon Line, Toei Mita Line, and Toei Shinjuku Line. Download a map (in Japanese) at http://jimbou.info/news/161005.html

POP-UP BOOK TOWNS

For three days each August, empty spaces in town are turned into temporary bookshops, both new and secondhand.

Books are not the only things that can pop up; so can book towns. Vianden in Luxembourg has developed into what it describes as a *Cité littéraire*, putting on a yearly two-day book festival in September in Vianden Castle, where writer Victor Hugo lived and worked for several months.

Meanwhile Graiguenamanagh in County Kilkenny, Ireland, has been running since 2003. What started as a low-key trial weekend has now turned into a major gathering. Books are at the heart of the celebrations, but there is also local food produce and crafts, the Graiguenamanagh Brass Band, and a busking competition, in a purposely family-friendly atmosphere. For three days each August, empty spaces in town are turned into temporary bookshops, with special shops for children and local authors. Around 300 booksellers from Ireland and the UK descend on the town.

Similarly, the market town of Ennistymon in County Clare repurposes unused shops for its annual Book Town Festival, as well as setting up stalls in the Courthouse Gallery, a space for exhibition and cultural events, and the Teach Ceoil cultural centre, the former Church of St Andrews. The festival is held over the June Bank Holiday weekend, attracting around twenty booksellers and drawing major names to speak and perform, such as Irish poet and playwright Rita Ann Higgins.

The festival is run by independent bookshop and arts venue Scéal Eile Books, based in nearby Ennis, and The Salmon Bookshop and Literary Centre on Parliament Street. The latter sells a wide selection of new and used books and is also the home of Salmon Poetry, one of Ireland's leading literary publishers, which has been publishing poetry for more than thirty-five years.

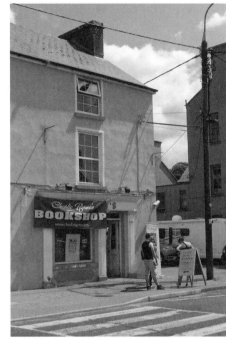

Above left: One woman in a boat (to say nothing of the dog) in Graiguenamanagh.

Below left: One of the many pop-up bookshops in Ennistymon.

Above right: Charlie Byrne's pop-up shop in Ennistymon.

Below right: The Salmon Bookshop in Ennistymon.

Brian Merriman

Brian Merriman (Brian Mac Giolla Meidhre) was an eighteenth-century Irish language poet best known for his 1000-line 'Cúirt An Mheán Oíche' ('The Midnight Court'), arguably the greatest comic poem in Irish literature. Merriman was probably born around 1747 in Ennistymon, where there is a statue in memory of his work.

Left: 'Life is too short to read a bad book' proclaims a floating bookshop in Graiguenamanagh.

Right: The statue of poet Brian Merriman in Ennistymon.

More information

- www.ennistymonbooks.com
- www.thesalmonbookshop.ie
- www.graiguenamanaghtownofbooks.com
- Vianden is an hour's drive from Luxembourg City. Graiguenamanagh is around two hours from Limerick, Cork and Dublin by road. The nearest station is Thomastown. Ennistymon is 70km south of Galway and an hour's drive from Limerick.

Picture credits

Every effort has been made to credit all copyright holders. The publishers will be glad to make good in future editions any ommissions brought to their attention.

© Agnes Niessou 19 below left and right

© Ajuntament d'Esplugues de Llobregat 23 above left

© AkhileshDasgupta 165

Alamy Stock Photo: Giles Targat 2; Michael Nicholson/DK 30 above; Emma Frater 31 right; frans lemmens 34 above, 35 above right; Martin Dr.Schulte-Kellinghaus 40, 42 above, 43 left; archphotography 46 above left; Arterra Picture Library 46 above right, 109 above left and below right; Christian Goupi 57; STOCKFOLIO 559 59 above; Jannis Werner 60; Ian Dagnall 63 below left and right; Aurora Photos 63 below middle; P Tomlins 67 above left; Vespasian 72 right; David Burton 86; Clare Gainey 92 left; Hemis 94; dov makabaw 101; Paul Boyes 121 above; Efrain Padro 124;

Naeblys 127 below right; Steve Skjold 135; Pekka Liukkonen 139 above left; South West Images Scotland 152; DGB 157 below; CHROMORANGE/Monika Wirth 159; Skye Hohmann 162; Arunabh Bhattacharjee 165; Idealink Photography 168; World Discovery 179 below left; Iain Masterton 179 below right; Sérgio Nogueira 188–189; Angela Hampton Picture Library 191

© Alina Golovachenko 38, 39 above and below left, 188–189

© Ammar Hassan 59 below

© Another Believer 131

© Antonio Tajuelo 179 above right

© Ap te Winkel 34 below

© Archmedus 35 above left and below right

© Associazione Le Maestà di Montereggio 6, 88, 89

© ATOUT FRANCE 58

© Audrey 127 above left

© Biswarup Ganguly 174 below middle

© Bjørn 55 above right

© Bobak Ha'Eri 134 above

© Boligbygg 85 below right

© Book House Foresta 105 above right

© Borrby Bokby 26, 27 below left and right

© Brian Elbourn 122 left and middle, 123

© Brian Lauer 127 below left

© Bücherstadt-Tourismus 160 below left and right, 161 right

© Byre Books 156

© Céline Huet 18 below

© Chocat Lyonel/Destination Saône-et-Loire 43 right

© Cité de l'Ecrit Montmorillon, 91, 92 below right

© Claire Tweed 55 left

© Clint Crawley 31 left

© Cristian Seel/velbert.de 81 below right

© Dave Collier 119

© Diana & Bill Adams 72 below left

© Don Dales 73 above

© Ed Kohler 134 below right

© Ed Webster 45

© Elmar Lamers 80 above right, 81 above right

© Emma Balch 10, 69 above, 96, 170 left and middle, 171

Picture credits

© Felisa Ramos Cruz 150 above left

© Fidel Raso 150 below right

© Fredrik Rubensson 27 above

© Geoff Walker 50

Getty Images: John Hay 36; P A Thompson 64; Jens Schlueter 78; THEGIFT777 111

© Hans Blossey/velbert.de 81 left

© Hans Josef Altmann 80 above left

© Heleen van Duin 173, 174 left, 175 above

© Helge Høifødt 147 above left

© Ingstrup Bogby 143 right

© Jan Kløvstad 54, 147 below right, 161 left

© Jayne Baldwin 155 below left

© Jean Blanquart 19 above

© Jessie Lendennie 182 below right

© JongOh Kim 105 below left, 105 below right

© José Luis Cernadas 149

© José Manuel Diogo 100 above

© J Waller 160 above left

© Kevin Hale 49

© Kreis Mettmann/Martina Chardin 80 below

© Kyungsub Shin 102

© La Coopérative-Collection Cérès Franco 97

© Lennart Brorsson 24

© Librería Alcuino Caligrafía & Arte 150 below left

© Lilleputthammer Lekeland 83, 84, 85 above and below left

© Lucas Daglio and Guada Boocles/stayhungrystayfoolish.es 20, 23 right

© Lysippos 117 above right

© Manuel Uzcanga 151

© Mark M Rogers 71

© Martin O'Brien 182 above left, 183 left

© Matt Sachtler 52

© Michael Drysdale 112

© Michelle Huggleston 68

© Monte Verità 13 above left

© Mysteries & More 73 below

© Norbert Lambart/Brittany Regional Council 17, 18 above

© Odean Long 130 right

© Olafur Thorisson 126

© Open Book 155 above left, 157 above

© Oshokim 105 above left

© Pete Monk 51 above

© Photoval/www.village-du-livre.ch 117 above and below left

© Pradipta Basu 175 below

© R-Store/Book and Bed 179 above left

© Rachel Watson 72 above, 184

© Rajib Ghosh 174 below right REX/Shutterstock: Environmental Images/Universal Images Group 141; Divyakant Solanki/EPA 166, 167

© Roberto Fiadone 170 right

© Rolf Plant 142, 143 left and middle

Author Biography

Alex Johnson is a journalist, blogger and the author of *A Book of Book Lists*, *Improbable Libraries*, *Bookshelf*, and *Shedworking: The Alternative Workplace Revolution*. He runs the web sites Shedworking at www.shedworking.co.uk and Bookshelf at www.onthebookshelf.co.uk.
Alex lives in St Albans with his wife, three children, and plenty of books from all over the world.

Page 184: A cosy riverside reading corner in Liberty Rock Books, Hobart, New York.

Page 188–189: The eclectic interior of a bookshop in Óbidos, Portugal, selling everything from books and CDs to tee-shirts and tote bags.

Opposite: Weathered book spines decorate a windowbox in Wigtown, Scotland.

Back cover, clockwise from top left: Book stalls in the grounds of Hay Castle, Hay-on-Wye, Wales; honestly bookshelves in Bredevoort, Netherlands; a barn-cum-bookshop in Hobart, New York; Les Chats Noirs in Cuisery.

TOMLINE

T... ...
Cost...

GE
RES

ON

ED

& Co.

BAILEY

Kenneth
Roberts

COLLINS

Thesaurus of
English Words
and Phrases

LONGMANS
1724

The
HOURS
and the
CENTURIES

PETER DE
MENDELSSOHN

THE
BODLEY HEAD

Krystia -1

Witold Nowak-Soliński

CIVIL ENGINEERING TODAY

OXFORD

...MOND

First Published in 2018 by Frances Lincoln,
an imprint of The Quarto Group.
The Old Brewery, 6 Blundell Street,
London N7 9BH, United Kingdom.
T (0)20 7700 6700; F (0)20 7700 8066
www.QuartoKnows.com

A catalogue record for this book is available from
the British Library.

ISBN 978 0 7112 3893 0

Printed and bound in China

3 4 5 6 7 8 9

MIX
Paper from
responsible sources
FSC® C104723

Brimming with creative inspiration, how-to projects and useful
information to enrich your everyday life, Quarto Knows is a
favourite destination for those pursuing their interests and passions.
Visit our site and dig deeper with our books into your area of interest:
Quarto Creates, Quarto Cooks, Quarto Homes, Quarto Lives,
Quarto Drives, Quarto Explores, Quarto Gifts, or Quarto Kids.